Iraq

Iraq

BY BYRON AUGUSTIN
AND JAKE KUBENA

*Enchantment of the World
Second Series*

Children's Press®

A Division of Scholastic Inc.

NEW YORK   TORONTO   LONDON   AUCKLAND   SYDNEY
MEXICO CITY   NEW DELHI   HONG KONG
DANBURY, CONNECTICUT

Frontispiece: Shepherds with their sheep in northern Iraq

Consultant: Peter Sluglett, Professor of Middle Eastern History, University of Utah,
Salt Lake City, Utah

Please note: All statistics are as up-to-date as possible at the time of publication.

Book production by Herman Adler Design

Library of Congress Cataloging-in-Publication Data

Iraq / by Byron Augustin and Jake Kubena.— Rev. ed.
    p. cm. — (Enchantment of the world)
  Includes index.
  ISBN 0-516-24852-9
  1. Iraq—Juvenile literature. I. Kubena, Jake. II. Title. III. Series.
  DS70.62.A84 2006
  956.7—dc22   2005032181

Acknowledgments

We would like to acknowledge the assistance provided by Mr. Mickey Hubicsak regarding photo research and the current situation in Iraq. We would also like to acknowledge our families for their support during the project.

This book is dedicated to the hope that the people of Iraq will have the opportunity to live in peace and prosperity. It is also dedicated to Dr. Lawrence Estaville, a remarkable scholar, a dynamic leader, and a cherished friend, and to Rebecca for too many reasons to mention. Finally, we dedicate the book to Lee and Debbie Seale-Kubena, who have provided loving support for a son to pursue his educational goals.

Cover photo:
Iraqi boy

Contents

Mosul

Young Iraqis

Cradle of Civilization

THE MODERN STATE OF IRAQ IS IN ITS INFANCY WHEN compared to many other countries. It was founded as a nation in 1920, after World War I. During its short existence, Iraq has experienced colonial rule, a monarchy, military coups, assassinations, dictatorships, foreign invasions, occupation troops, and a transitional government. Iraq's citizens have paid a heavy price for their nation's involvement in recent wars. The Iraqi economy has also suffered from the ravages of military conflict. At the same time, Iraqis are understandably proud of their rich history and cultural heritage. They are a strong people who cling to the hope that the future will bring peace and prosperity.

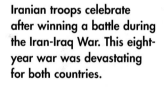

Opposite: **The colorful dome and minaret of a mosque rise above the Square of the Unknown Soldier in Baghdad.**

Iranian troops celebrate after winning a battle during the Iran-Iraq War. This eight-year war was devastating for both countries.

The roots of civilization reach deep into the fabric of Iraq's culture. Southern Iraq was the location of one of the first permanent settlements of early humans. The Sumerians built cities in the Tigris and Euphrates river valleys more than five thousand years ago. The flooding rivers provided rich soil for agriculture. The rivers also served as a source of freshwater both to drink and to irrigate crops. Traders, too, used the rivers to transport goods. Through the years, many different groups of people and empires flourished in this region, called the "Cradle of Civilization."

Nippur was a religious center during Sumerian times. Six-thousand-year-old ruins have been uncovered there.

Over the centuries, many powerful empires also laid claim to what is now Iraq. These include the Sumerians, Akkadians, Babylonians, Assyrians, Persians, Greeks, Arabs, and Ottomans. Powerful rulers such as Sargon I, Hammurabi II, Sennacherib, Nebuchadnezzar II, Cyrus the Great, Alexander the Great, Abu'l-Abbas, Hulagu Khan, and Suleiman the Magnificent all left their mark on the region.

Remarkable cities such as Ur, Babylon, Nineveh, Ctesiphon, and Baghdad grew to be some of the greatest urban centers in the world. Huge advances were made in architecture, science, medicine, mathematics, writing, and art. In the Islamic Middle Ages, Iraq was home to some of the world's earliest universities and best libraries.

Sargon I founded the Akkadian Empire. He ruled in the 2300s B.C.

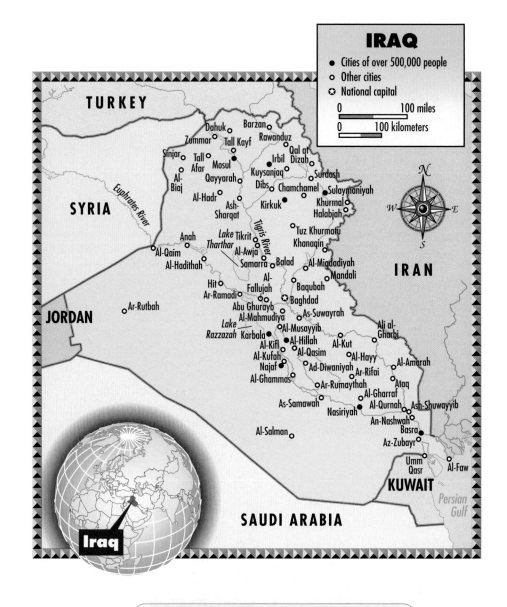

TURKEY

SYRIA

JORDAN

IRAN

SAUDI ARABIA

KUWAIT

Persian Gulf

Euphrates River

Tigris River

Dahuk
Barzan
Zummar
Rawanduz
Tall Kayf
Sinjar
Tall Afar
Qal at Dizah
Irbil
Mosul
Kuysanjaq
Surdash
Al-Biaj
Qayyarah
Dibs
Chamchamel
Sulaymaniyah
Al-Hadr
Kirkuk
Khurmal
Ash-Sharqat
Halabjah
Anah
Lake Tharthar
Tikrit
Tuz Khurmatu
Al-Awja
Khanaqin
Al-Qaim
Samarra
Balad
Al-Hadithah
Al-Miqdadiyah
Mandali
Hit
Al-Fallujah
Baqubah
Ar-Ramadi
Abu Ghurayb
Baghdad
Ar-Rutbah
Al-Mahmudiya
As-Suwayrah
Lake Razzazah
Al-Musayyib
Ali al-Gharbi
Karbala
Al-Hillah
Al-Kut
Al-Kifl
Al-Qasim
Al-Hayy
Al-Kufah
Al-Amarah
Najaf
Ad-Diwaniyah
Ar-Rifai
Ataq
Al-Ghammas
Ar-Rumaythah
Al-Gharraf
As-Samawah
Al-Qurnah
Ash-Shuwayyib
Nasiriyah
An-Nashwah
Al-Salman
Basra
Az-Zubayr
Umm Qasr
Al-Faw

Iraq

The Lay of the Land

Most of Iraq is fairly flat. Occasionally, the surface is cut by deep, seasonal streambeds called wadis, which are usually dry. The wadis were created by the raging waters of flash floods after heavy rainfall. Northeastern Iraq offers a refreshing change in the landscape. There, some peaks of the Zagros Mountains rise to more than 10,000 feet (3,000 meters).

Living in Iraq can be like living in an oven. While the short winter may be mild, most of the year is unpleasantly hot. During the summers, temperatures rise above 100 degrees Fahrenheit (38 degrees Celsius) day after day. Rain during the summer months is almost nonexistent. During the summer, Iraqis face a near-constant haze and frequent blinding dust storms and sandstorms.

The Zagros Mountains rise in northeastern Iraq. This region is much cooler than the rest of the country.

Most Iraqis are Muslims, followers of the religion of Islam. For most Muslims, Islam is truly a way of life. Islam impacts their daily routine, food choices, marriage, divorce, education, political decisions, and death.

Iraq has the potential to be one of the wealthiest nations in the world. The country has large oil reserves, perhaps as much as 200 billion barrels. But recent governments have squandered much of the oil wealth on wars and their own luxurious lifestyle. New oil production has been hindered by a lack of research and development, aging equipment, and wars and strife. Today, the nation has a high level of poverty and massive international debt.

An oil refinery in Basra. Much of Iraq's oil equipment is old and in need of repairs.

The twenty-five-year dictatorial regime of Saddam Hussein continues to cast a dark cloud over Iraq's future. In 2003, coalition military forces, led by the United States and the United Kingdom, invaded Iraq and removed Hussein and his Ba'th Party from power. A transitional government is in place, but violence is common, and the citizens of Iraq are plagued by a lack of security. Distinct differences of opinion among and between Shi'i Muslims, Sunni Muslims, and Kurds make the formation of a legitimate democratic government difficult. The fate of Iraqis hangs by a fragile thread. Will the future bring peace and the creation of a legitimate government, or will it bring chaos and a potential civil war? The answer is difficult to predict, and only time will tell.

American soldiers on patrol in Iraq. Violence continued to be rampant after Saddam Hussein's regime was toppled.

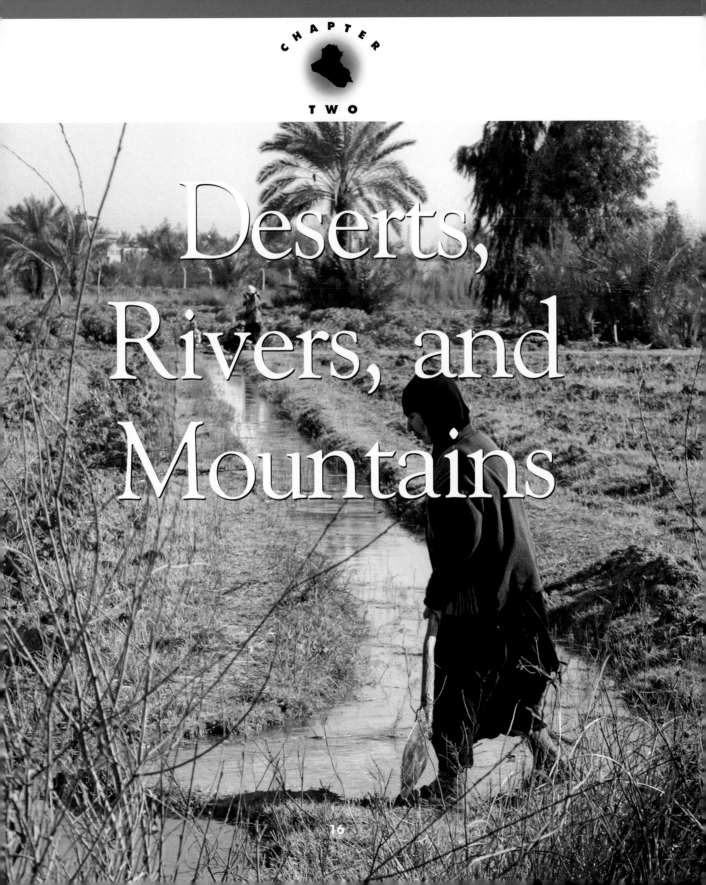

Deserts, Rivers, and Mountains

IRAQ HAS SOMETIMES BEEN CALLED THE "HEART OF THE Middle East." It is surrounded by six other nations of the Middle East, the part of the world where Africa and Asia meet. Iraq's two largest rivers and its major waterways, the Tigris and the Euphrates, carry water that sustains life throughout much of the region. A narrow coastline along Iraq's southeastern border provides a connection to one of the world's most strategic bodies of water, the Persian Gulf. The region has attracted human settlement for thousands of years.

Opposite: **A woman redirects water to her farm field in central Iraq.**

The Tigris River flows about 850 miles (1,400 km) across Iraq.

Iraq is roughly the shape of a piece of pie. It is widest along its northwestern border and narrows as it reaches the Persian Gulf in the southeast. The country covers an area of 169,235 square miles (438,317 square kilometers), which is slightly larger than the state of California. Iraq is almost completely surrounded by land, with the exception of a 36-mile (58 km) stretch of coastline along the northern edge of the Persian Gulf. The Tigris and the Euphrates flow all the way across

The Persian Gulf is an amazing sight from space. The space shuttle *Columbia* took this picture of the Strait of Hormuz (center) and the Persian Gulf (top).

Iraq's Geographic Features

Area: 169,235 square miles (438,317 sq km)

Highest Recorded Temperature: 124°F (51°C)

Lowest Recorded Temperature: 12°F (-11°C)

Highest Elevation: Haji Ibrahim, 11,834 feet (3,607 m)

Lowest Elevation: Sea level along the Persian Gulf

Longest Shared Border: 906 miles (1,458 km), with Iran

Major Port: Umm Qasr

Largest City: Baghdad

Largest Lake: Lake Tharthar

Largest Producing Oil Field: Rumaila (North and South Fields)

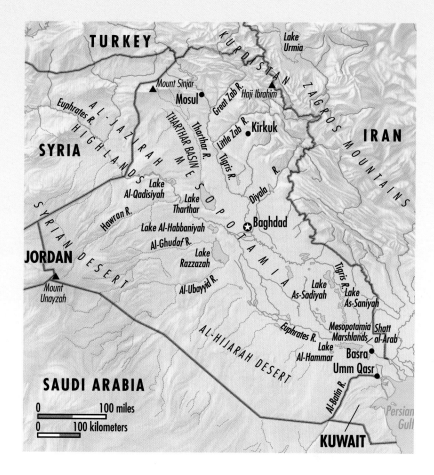

the country, from the north to the southeast, where they combine to form the Shatt al-Arab, which empties into the Persian Gulf.

Neighbors

Iraq shares borders with six nations. Iran is to the east, Saudi Arabia and Kuwait are to the south, Jordan and Syria are to the west, and Turkey is to the north. In recent times,

Grazing sheep are common in the foothills of the Zagros Mountains in northeastern Iraq.

Iraq and its neighbors have been in frequent conflict over its borders. In 1980, Iraq went to war with Iran over a border dispute along the Shatt al-Arab. There has also been consistent tension along the northern border with Turkey over issues related to the Kurds, an ethnic group that lives in both countries. In 1990, Iraq invaded Kuwait because of territorial claims.

Landform Regions

Most of Iraq is relatively flat and low, rarely rising to more than 1,000 feet (300 m) above sea level. The exception is in northeastern Iraq, where there are rolling hills and mountains. Iraq can be divided into four physical regions: the desert, the al-Jazirah highlands, the mountains, and the floodplains of the Tigris and Euphrates rivers.

The Desert

Approximately one-half of Iraq is covered by an inhospitable desert. The desert of western Iraq is part of the larger Syrian Desert, which spreads across parts of Syria, Jordan, and Saudi Arabia. This desert region slopes downward from the northwest. Along the western borders, elevations rise to about 2,000 feet (610 m). By the time the desert meets the Euphrates River in central Iraq, elevations of 100 to 300 feet (30 to 90 m) are common.

A Syrian soldier guards Syria's border with Iraq. The two countries share a 376 mile (605 km) border through mostly empty territory.

The desert plains in Iraq are composed of various types of rock. Much of the surface is made up of sand, gravel, flint, and chert. Occasionally, wadis are carved into the flat landscape. Most of the year, these wadis are totally dry. But thunderstorms sometimes produce extremely heavy rainfall in a short amount of time. This may result in flash floods that roar down the wadis, sometimes overflowing their banks. These flash floods can wash cars and trucks off roads as if they were toys.

The desert is a challenging environment for humans to live in. Because rainfall is so scarce, there is little natural vegetation. It is too dry for crops to grow, and even livestock find the desert a difficult place to live. The only human settlements are a few small villages.

A man tries to prevent his cart from being swept away during a flash flood near Kirkuk.

Few plants grow around Lake Tharthar, but the lake's waters are used to irrigate distant fields.

Al-Jazirah Highlands

Stretching north from Baghdad in central Iraq all the way to the Turkish border is a highland region known as al-Jazirah. In Arabic, *al-Jazirah* means "the island." This wedge of desert plateau lies between the Tigris and Euphrates rivers. The surface of the plateau is flat or gently rolling. Though this region is too dry for much human activity, parts of it are suitable for livestock grazing or growing grains such as wheat or barley.

Lake Tharthar, Iraq's largest lake, is located in al-Jazirah. The Iraqis have built a canal from the Tigris River to Lake Tharthar. During periods of flooding, water from the river is diverted into the basin around the lake, where few people live.

The north is the only mountainous part of Iraq. Near the Turkish border, elevations are higher than 7,000 feet (2,100 m) above sea level.

The Mountains

The rugged beauty of the mountains of northeastern Iraq is a remarkable contrast to the flatness of the rest of the country. In the far north, the mountains are an extension of Turkey's Taurus Mountain range. Along the border with Iran, the Zagros Mountains spill across the frontier into Iraq. The highest elevation in Iraq is Haji Ibrahim at 11,834 feet (3,607 m). Meltwater from the winter snows in the mountainous northeast provides much of the water for the rivers that flow into the Tigris River. In the early spring, this meltwater sometimes combines with the winter rainy season to produce disastrous flooding on the lower Tigris River.

The Floodplains

The area from Baghdad south to the Persian Gulf is one of the most famous regions in the world. It has been called one of the birthplaces of human civilization. Part of the Fertile Crescent, it has been a rich site of human settlement through the ages. Most important, it is a central part of a region known as Mesopotamia, or "the land between the rivers."

The fertile land near the Tigris and Euphrates rivers allowed the people of Mesopotamia to settle down and farm. This enabled human civilization to flourish.

Too Much Water

Both the Tigris and the Euphrates are prone to flooding during the early spring. These rivers have flooded for thousands of years. This is both a blessing and a curse. On the positive side, the floodwaters carry heavy loads of sand and silt, which make the soil more fertile. On the negative side, floods can produce walls of water that wreak havoc on cities and villages along the rivers.

Baghdad has been a frequent victim of flooding. In 1831, the Tigris River overflowed its banks, sweeping away more than fifteen thousand residents of Baghdad and most of the city's houses.

The Tigris and the Euphrates rivers were central to the rise of human civilization. As the rivers flooded over millions of years, they deposited rich silt and sand, creating a broad plain with fertile soil where crops could be grown. The floodplains also contain intertwining river channels, irrigation canals, lakes, and wetlands. In arid regions such as Iraq, water is a precious resource. The abundant water in the floodplains of the Tigris and the Euphrates allowed humanity to thrive.

Women collect water during the hot summer, when the temperature frequently tops 120°F (49°C).

Hot and Dry

Iraq's climate can be brutal. During the summers, temperatures across most of the country rise above 100°F (38°C) on a regular basis. Many places in Iraq have recorded temperatures above 120°F (49°C). The record temperature for Iraq is 124°F (51°C). During the hot summers, strong winds sometimes whip up dust storms and sandstorms.

Temperatures cool during the winter months, but freezing temperatures are extremely rare in Iraq. Frost seldom occurs more than five days each year. In the south, some years are frost free. Iraq's lowest recorded temperature is 12°F (-11°C), at al-Salman.

A Wall of Dust and Sand

Every summer, Iraqis endure choking dust storms and sandstorms. Most of the country receives very little rain from June through September, and extremely high temperatures dry out the soil. Winds with speeds of up to 50 miles per hour (80 kph) lift the dust and sand high in the air, forming a wall that may stretch 5,000 feet (1,500 m) toward the sky. These storms roll across the landscape with a suffocating effect. When these storms hit, people may be able to see only a few feet (1 to 3 m) down the road. Airports shut down, and cars slow to a crawl. Most people stay inside, waiting for the storm to pass.

The mountains of northern Iraq are by far the coldest part of the country. In the mountains' higher reaches, snow covers the ground several months during the year.

Parts of spring and fall can be pleasant, but they are brief. The northeastern uplands and mountains have a more agreeable climate than the rest of Iraq. In this region, temperatures are more moderate, winters are wet, and summers are dry.

Precipitation is scarce across much of the country, especially in the summer. Most weather stations record an average of less than 6 inches (15 centimeters) of precipitation each year. Almost all of it comes as rainfall, but the mountains along the borders with Turkey and Iran can receive heavy snowfall.

A Look at Iraq's Cities

Mosul (above) is Iraq's second-largest city, with an estimated population of 1,739,000 in 2002. It is located on the banks of the Tigris River. The average January temperature in Mosul is 44°F (7°C), and the average July temperature is 91°F (33°C). Mosul contains the highest percentage of Christians of all Iraqi cities. Christian churches dating back to the ninth century are popular tourist attractions.

The city of Basra (right) was founded in 636. Today, it is the third-largest city in Iraq with a population of 1,337,000. Basra is located along the banks of the Shatt al-Arab at an elevation of 7 feet (2 m) above sea level. The average January temperature is 54°F (12°C), while the average July temperature is a stifling 96°F (36°C). The city is located in the center of a fertile agricultural area.

A Struggle
to Survive

The desert is home to many kinds of scorpions. Some can grow up to 8 inches (20 cm) long.

Because so much of Iraq is covered by desert, it is one of the least hospitable places in the world for plants and animals to live. They must be specially adapted to the desert in order to survive. While much of Iraq appears to be uninhabited by plants and animals, in fact life prevails across the desert and in the rest of the nation.

Life in the Desert

All desert plants must be able to live with a very small amount of rain. They must use the available moisture efficiently and conserve it through long periods of total drought. The Iraqi desert is home to grasses, small bushes, and vines that can all survive long periods without rain.

Opposite: **Water buffalo cross a muddy river in southern Iraq.**

A Desert Delicacy

Desert truffles are one of the most unusual foods eaten in Iraq. They are a type of fungus related to mushrooms. The truffles begin life as tiny spores that grow into long invisible threads. These threads attach themselves to the root system of a rockrose bush and wait for just the right climatic conditions. Rain must come in October or November, and just the right amount must fall. The rain must be accompanied by lightning—the more the better. The lightning triggers a chemical reaction that produces nitrogen. This nitrogen encourages the truffles to grow.

By March or April, the truffles have grown to the size of small potatoes or golf balls. In fact, some desert dwellers call these truffles "the potatoes of thunder." Experienced truffle hunters know just where to look for desert truffles, but they guard these locations like hidden treasure. Desert truffles are loaded with protein, and they are frequently cooked over a charcoal fire in place of meat.

Desert plants use different techniques to survive. Some have a deep taproot that reaches water far below the surface. Others have a shallow root system that spreads many feet on each side to capture precious moisture after rain. Most have specific cells that store water. Their leaves are usually small so that they do not lose much water from evaporation. Others have leaves with waxy surfaces or small hairs that also decrease water loss.

Geckos, Rodents, and Snakes

Animals must meet many of the same challenges as plants if they are to survive in the deserts of Iraq. Because rain is so rare, desert animals get much of the moisture that they need from the vegetation and other animals that they eat. To escape the scorching daytime heat, most animals are nocturnal, coming out only at night. During the day, they burrow in the sand or seek the shade of plant life.

Reptiles and rodents are the most common animals found in the desert. Iraq is home to several species of lizards. One of the most interesting is the leopard gecko, which comes in a variety of colors including brown, yellow, tangerine,

Leopard geckos live in the rocky desert. They spend the hot days in the shade of rocks and then come out at night to hunt insects and spiders.

Jerboas are well-adapted to the desert. They get all the water they need from the food they eat, so they do not need to drink.

gold, black, and white. After leopard geckos shed their skin, they eat it as a source of protein. They are about 8 inches (20 cm) long, including the tail.

The desert is home to several species of snakes, many of which are poisonous. The most dangerous is the saw-scale viper. Many scientists consider it the most dangerous snake in the world. It is aggressive, and its venom is extremely toxic. The viper will sometimes strike without being provoked and will occasionally chase its victims. Its bite often results in death.

There are also several dangerous spiders, centipedes, and scorpions in the desert. Their bites or stings can cause burning, swelling, vomiting, sweating, and muscle spasms. One species of scorpion has a venom that can lead to death within two to twenty hours. It is always wise to check your boots or shoes before putting them on in the desert.

The jerboa is one of Iraq's most unusual rodents. Its hind legs are long in proportion to its body, and it hops like a kangaroo. A jerboa can jump 6 feet (2 m) in a single leap.

The National Bird

The chukar is the national bird of Iraq. Chukars are about 1 foot (30 cm) long. Their feathers are usually several different colors, including light brown, creamy white, gray, chestnut, and black. The bird is best known for its loud, crackling call that it repeats rapidly. Chukars are found in flocks of up to forty birds. Chukars, which look something like quails, are prized by hunters and can be a delicious meal.

Large mammals are scarce in the Iraqi desert. While a few herds of sand gazelles survive, most other species have been hunted into extinction.

Life in the Mountains

The northeast is the only part of Iraq that gets enough precipitation for trees to grow. Ten thousand years ago, dense stands of oak, cedar, pine, and poplar blanketed the mountain slopes. At that time, 13 percent of Iraq was forested, but today, timber cutting has reduced that number to less than 2 percent. Oak is the only major species still found in significant numbers. Fruit and nut trees, harvested for commercial use, have replaced most of the native trees.

Traditional Healers

The people of Iraq who use plants as medicine are called *attars*, or traditional healers. Iraqi scientists have identified almost one hundred medicinal plants used by these healers.

Most of the more widely used plants are found in the mountains. Wormwood vapor is used to treat coughing and diabetes. Ephedrine, from the plant ephedra foliata, is used to cure asthma and other respiratory illnesses. Attars treat joint swelling with five different plants.

Unfortunately, the knowledge of the attars is seldom passed on to the next generation, and their skills may soon die out and be forgotten.

The mountains are the only region in Iraq where large animals survive in significant numbers. Magnificent bighorn sheep can sometimes be spotted on high ridges. Hyenas, wolves, and wild pigs are also found in the mountains, as are large birds such as eagles, hawks, vultures, and owls.

Life in the River Valleys

The most densely populated part of Iraq is the lower valley of the Tigris and the Euphrates rivers. Humans first settled there at least eight thousand years ago. Its long history of human settlement has also caused the destruction of most of the region's native plants and animals.

Today, the floodplains reveal a dense network of irrigation and drainage canals, cultivated fields, and rural villages. Farmers produce rice, wheat, barley, vegetables, cotton, dates, and livestock.

Wheat is the most common grain grown in Iraq. But wheat production has dropped dramatically in recent years because of drought, declining soil quality, and war and upheaval.

The activities of humans in recent years have been disastrous for the Iraqi environment. Over the past twenty-five years, Iraq has been involved in three destructive wars. War can be devastating to the environment. In Iraq, chemical plants, oil refineries, and other industrial sites have been bombed, releasing massive amounts of toxic materials into the environment. Military vehicles have left scars on the surface of the desert that may take hundreds of years to heal. Crushing the fragile surface of the thin desert soils causes it to erode, or wear away, more quickly. This erosion has helped increase dust storms and sandstorms. In addition, an estimated ten million landmines

The Date Palm

The date palm has grown in Mesopotamia for fifty million years. Many experts believe that it was the first domesticated agricultural plant. Tablets dating back to 2500 B.C. mention the date palm as a cultivated tree. Today, millions of date palms are grown in Iraq, which is one of the top three date producers in the world. The date is an important part of Arab culture, and the fruit is frequently served to visitors with coffee or tea. It has a high calorie content and provides a boost of energy.

The Baghdad Zoo

Until 2003, when the United States led an invasion of Iraq, the Baghdad Zoo was the largest zoo in the Middle East, home to more than six hundred animals. Unfortunately, there was heavy fighting near the zoo, and it sustained considerable damage. After that, looters stole any creatures they could. By the time they were done, only fifty animals remained at the zoo. Veterinarians from around the world offered to help the animals still there. Recently, American military personnel and civilian engineers have helped rebuild the zoo complex, and it is once again open for visitors.

Before Saddam Hussein had the marshes drained, the Marsh Arabs used boats to travel around their village.

have been planted in the ground in Iraq. These mines blow up when they are stepped on, so they pose a threat to both humans and animals.

The brutal regime of Saddam Hussein had little interest in environmental protection. Irrigation and drainage projects approved while he was in power resulted in disastrous increases in the salt content of Iraq's best farmland. His political decisions were frequently motivated by personal hatred. In 1991, the Marsh Arabs, who lived in the wetlands of the lower Tigris-Euphrates valley, rebelled against his rule. To punish them, he had the marshes where they lived drained, destroying the largest area of natural wetlands in the Middle East.

Iraqi citizens must also share some of the blame for environmental damage. Farmers have used poor irrigation methods that have damaged the soil. In the country's arid and semiarid regions, they have allowed livestock to overgraze on the sparse vegetation. In the mountains, most of the trees have been cut down for firewood or lumber.

Iraq's natural environment is also threatened by actions outside the country's borders. Both the Tigris and the Euphrates rivers begin in Turkey, and the Euphrates also flows through Syria. Large dam projects in both Turkey and Syria have substantially reduced the flow of water in these two critical rivers. The low water flow is already creating a crisis in Iraq's most important agricultural area.

Destroying Paradise

The Mesopotamian marshlands lie just to the north of Basra. Prior to 1991, they were the largest natural wetlands in the Middle East. This series of freshwater lakes, swamps, marshes, and seasonally flooded plains extended over more than 37,000 acres (15,000 hectares). Wild water buffalo, otters, and wild boar lived in the marshes. They roamed freely among the aquatic plants such as reeds, rushes, and papyrus. Thousands of migratory birds wintered in the wetlands or stopped to rest on their way between Asia and Africa. It was a water paradise.

The Marsh Arabs (Ma'dan) and their ancestors have lived in these rich wetlands for more than five thousand years. After the 1991 Gulf War, the Marsh Arabs rebelled against Saddam Hussein's dictatorial rule. He responded by destroying the natural habitat necessary for their lifestyle. Hussein had the wetlands drained, wiping out much of the plant and animal life. This was one of the most serious attacks on the natural environment in world history. Hussein also massacred thousands of Marsh Arabs and drove most of those who survived into exile.

After Saddam Hussein was removed from power in 2003, an international effort to restore the wetlands was begun. Currently, about one-third of the region has been returned to wetlands. Restoring the remaining area will be a long, expensive process. Yet perhaps one day this Garden of Eden will again flourish.

Reflections
in Time

I RAQ'S HISTORY STRETCHES BACK FARTHER THAN THAT OF almost any other nation. It is a story of grandeur, destruction, rebirth, and political intrigue. In the end, it is nothing short of fascinating.

Ancient Sumer

Sumer was the first great civilization of Mesopotamia. The Sumerians lived along the marshes and channels of the Tigris and the Euphrates rivers in what is now southern Iraq. Around 3500 B.C., the Sumerians began to develop agricultural technology that would forever change how humans lived. They built simple but effective irrigation systems that increased food production by expanding the fields into the desert. The Sumerians also invented a copper plow and later a bronze plow that allowed them to farm additional land. Many historians also believe that the Sumerians invented and perfected the wheel.

These new technologies greatly increased agricultural production.

The Sumerians invented both the wheel and the plow.

This allowed some Sumerians to abandon farming and develop some of the world's first urban settlements. These urban Sumerians became craftspeople, merchants, traders, engineers, and scribes.

The scribes developed one of the most important elements of human civilization: a system of writing called cuneiform.

The Sumerians' writing system is believed to have been the first of its kind in the world. The scribes etched the symbols into soft clay tablets. Some of these tablets, which were recovered at sites in Mesopotamia, provide the first written history of early human civilization.

The Sumerians built cities along the floodplains of the Tigris and the Euphrates. One Sumerian city, Ur, is believed to have been home to thirty thousand people.

The success of the Sumerians did not go unnoticed. Warlike tribes invaded the region, captured the cities, and killed the Sumerian leaders. The most powerful invader was Sargon I from ancient Akkad. He fought many battles and eventually united most of Mesopotamia under his rule. His descendants ruled from 2302 B.C. to 2108 B.C.

Babylonia

The Kingdom of Babylonia resulted from the merging of the Sumerian and Akkadian cultures. The city of Babylon became the capital of southern Mesopotamia. Babylon was one of the greatest urban centers in the history of the world. The city covered several square miles. It was enclosed by massive walls 50 feet (15 m) high and 55 feet (17 m) thick. A moat in front of the walls provided additional protection.

Walls of the ancient city of Babylon still stand today. The city was built along the banks of the Euphrates River.

The city of Babylon flourished for almost two thousand years. It was a center of trade, manufacturing, education, medicine, and above all, agricultural engineering. One of the earliest and greatest leaders of Babylon was Hammurabi.

Hammurabi ruled Babylon during the mid-eighteenth century B.C. He was a brilliant military strategist and administrator. He developed one of the earliest legal codes, called the Code of Hammurabi, known to experts. The Code of Hammurabi, which included both the laws and the punishments for breaking them, was etched into a stone tablet and put on display for all to see.

The boundaries of Babylonia shifted over the years. The kingdom's prosperity often attracted the attention of outsiders who wanted to control the region and its riches. Hittites, Hurrians, Kassites, and Assyrians all invaded Babylonia and gained some measure of control.

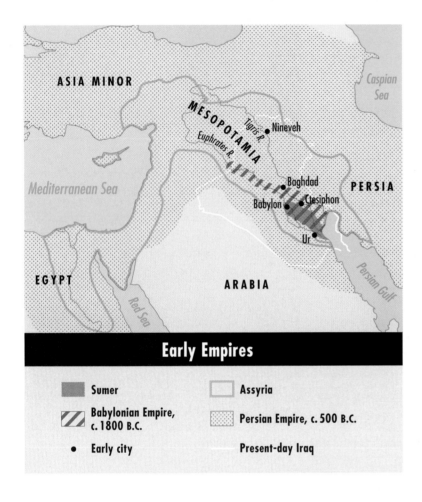

Early Empires

- **Sumer**
- **Babylonian Empire, c. 1800 B.C.**
- • **Early city**
- **Assyria**
- **Persian Empire, c. 500 B.C.**
- **Present-day Iraq**

The most successful invaders were the Assyrians, who controlled northern Mesopotamia from the ancient city of Nineveh, in what is now Mosul. The reign of the Assyrian king Sennacherib (705–681 B.C.) was particularly brutal for Babylon. Under his rule, the Assyrians destroyed the city of Babylon and slaughtered most of its inhabitants. Streams of blood flowed through the city, and corpses were stacked in huge piles. Buildings were destroyed, temples ransacked, and most of the wealth of the city was looted. Babylon, the great city, lay in ruin.

A Rebirth

During the reign of King Nebuchadnezzar II (605–562 B.C.) Babylon rose from the ashes to new grandeur. Nebuchadnezzar helped the Babylonians to regain control over most of Mesopotamia. He was a great warrior, a brilliant statesman, and an amazing rebuilder.

The Hanging Gardens of Babylon

The Hanging Gardens of Babylon are one of the Seven Wonders of the Ancient World. The gardens are said to have been built by King Nebuchadnezzar II for his wife, Queen Amytis. According to legend, the queen was a native of a land that was cool and well-watered. The king reportedly built the gardens to remind his wife of her homeland.

No clear-cut scientific evidence proves the existence of the gardens, but ancient historians wrote elaborate descriptions of them. They told of many levels of terraces covered with stately trees and beautiful flowering plants. The gardens are believed to have had a complex irrigation system to lift water to the highest level. Small canals then channeled the water to the lush plants that were growing in a desert.

His greatest accomplishment was the restoration of Babylon. New buildings sprang up across the city. Temples, palaces, and markets were scattered throughout. The bricks used in the construction process were frequently covered with beautiful enamel tiles. Many of the bricks were stamped with the words "I am Nebuchadnezzar, King of Babylon."

After King Nebuchadnezzar II died, the glory of Babylon faded rapidly. Without strong leadership, the military began to fall apart. The weakened condition of the army attracted the attention of Cyrus the Great of Persia. In 538 B.C., he entered the gates of Babylon with little resistance. For the next two centuries, the Persians were in control.

The Entrance of Alexander into Babylon, by Charles Le Brun. Alexander triumphantly took control of Babylon after defeating the Persians.

The Greeks

When Alexander the Great (356–323 B.C.) inherited the throne of Macedonia—a country that had just gained control of all of Greece—at the age of twenty, the world was about to change forever. Many historians believe that Alexander had the most brilliant military mind in world history. He soon turned his attention to the Persians, whom he hated for invading Greece 150 years earlier.

In 331 B.C., Alexander conquered the Persian Empire, which included Mesopotamia. However, Alexander died at the age of thirty-three in Babylon, and without his dynamic leadership, the Greeks would rule the area for only a short time. Control of Babylonia shifted among several groups. Finally, the Sassanid Dynasty of Persia took control of Mesopotamia in A.D. 226. They established their capital in Ctesiphon, approximately 20 miles (30 km) south of present-day Baghdad. They maintained control for several hundred years, but they were difficult years marked by assassinations and unrest.

The Arabs

Events to the west would soon change life in Mesopotamia. Muhammad, the prophet of the religion of Islam, died in 632 in what is now Saudi Arabia. By the time he died, Muslims—followers of Islam—had gained control of the Arabian Peninsula. Within a year, the Arabs were preparing to spread their new faith across vast new territories. In 633, they began to make raids into Mesopotamia, and they soon engaged the Sassanid Persians in bloody battles. In 651, the last of the Sassanid Persian emperors was killed. The Arab armies spread over all of Mesopotamia. A new era had begun. Henceforth, the people of ancient Mesopotamia would speak Arabic and follow the religion of Islam.

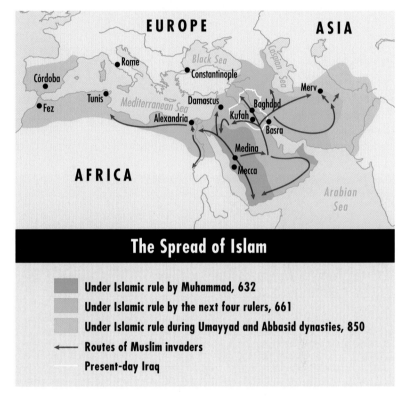

The Spread of Islam

Under Islamic rule by Muhammad, 632
Under Islamic rule by the next four rulers, 661
Under Islamic rule during Umayyad and Abbasid dynasties, 850
Routes of Muslim invaders
Present-day Iraq

Islamic Leadership

Islam was not without controversy in these early years. At the time of Muhammad's death, a new leader needed to be selected. Some followers preferred a blood relative, represented by Ali ibn Abu Talib, Muhammad's cousin and son-in-law. Others supported Muhammad's companion Abu Bakr. The controversy over who should lead Islam resulted in a major split among the faithful. Those who supported Ali were called the Shi'is, which means "Partisans of Ali." The other group would come to be known as the Sunnis.

In the end, Abu Bakr was chosen, and he was given the title Caliph of Islam. He was succeeded by Umar, Uthman, and eventually Ali. Ali attempted to establish the capital of Islam in al-Kufah, in present-day Iraq. He worked desperately

Abu Bakr Muhammad ibn Zakariya, the leader of Islamic medicine, works in his laboratory in Baghdad.

to hold the faithful together, but he had many powerful enemies, and in January 661, Ali was murdered. The Syrian governor, Mu'awiyah, claimed the caliphate and moved Islam's capital to Damascus in Syria. This was the beginning of the Umayyad Dynasty.

Mu'awiyah proved to be an able administrator. When he died in 680, his son Yazid claimed the caliphate. The Shi'i of Iraq favored Hussein, Ali's son and the grandson of Muhammad. They invited Hussein to leave Mecca in what is now Saudi Arabia and restore the leadership of Islam in al-Kufah.

On the trip to Iraq from Mecca, Hussein and a small band of followers were surrounded by four thousand soldiers who had been sent by Yazid. Hussein refused to surrender, and he and most of his group were massacred near the city of Karbala, Iraq. Karbala remains the holiest city of Shi'i Muslims, and thousands make annual pilgrimages to honor Hussein's death.

The Abbasid Dynasty

In 750, the center of Islamic power shifted back to Iraq and the city of Baghdad. The new caliph was Abu'l-Abbas, a descendant of one of Muhammad's uncles. Under the Abbasids, Baghdad became the intellectual capital of the world. One of the first universities in the world was constructed. Students studied mathematics, physics, medicine, philosophy, and astronomy. The region prospered, becoming a dominant political and economic force for five hundred years.

The Mongols

In the early thirteenth century, Mongol invaders swept out of China and into Mesopotamia. In 1258, Hulagu Khan, a grandson of the great Mongol leader Genghis Khan, entered Baghdad with two hundred thousand troops. What took place next can be matched by few events in world history. The Mongols murdered every human being they could find. In a matter of a few days, an estimated eight hundred thousand citizens of Baghdad were slaughtered. Once again, the brilliant lights of one of Mesopotamia's most glorious civilizations had been snuffed out.

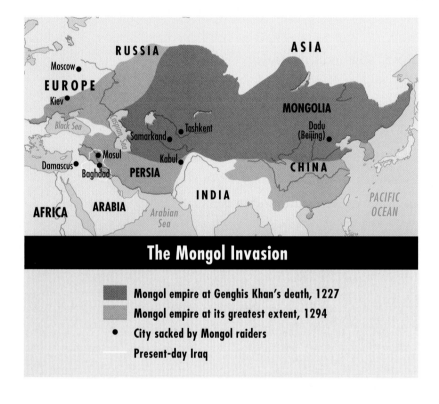

The Mongol Invasion

■ Mongol empire at Genghis Khan's death, 1227
■ Mongol empire at its greatest extent, 1294
● City sacked by Mongol raiders
— Present-day Iraq

The Ottoman Turks

Chaos followed the Mongol invasion, as various groups tried to control the region. First, the Mongol conqueror Tamerlane invaded. Later, the Persian Safavid Dynasty gained control. The Safavids adopted Shi'ism as their official religion, and they persecuted Sunni religious leaders. This caught the attention of Suleiman the Magnificent, the Ottoman sultan. In 1534, he organized an army that conquered the Safavids in Iraq. Ottoman rule lasted until 1918, the end of World War I.

By the time the Ottoman Turks gained control of Mesopotamia, they ruled a vast empire. They paid little attention to the distant provinces of Iraq. The region slipped into poverty, and the Turks left the people alone as long as they paid their taxes. For the most part, Iraq governed itself, with the daily tasks of bureaucracy in the hands of the more educated Sunni population. While the Ottoman Turks were losing interest in Iraq, other European powers were preparing to step in and fill the void.

During the rule of Suleiman the Magnificent, the Ottomans took control of Baghdad. Suleiman was known as a fair and tolerant ruler and a great supporter of the arts.

The British had a long history of influence in the Persian Gulf, largely motivated by their substantial investments in India. India also provided a huge market for British goods. Connecting the Persian Gulf to an overland route through Iraq and on into western Europe was a high priority for the British. The Germans were also interested in the region. They wanted to build a railroad that would connect Berlin and Baghdad.

World War I broke out in 1914. Great Britain, France, and Russia were the leaders of the so-called Allies. They were fighting the Central Powers, which included Germany and Austria-Hungary. When the war began, the Ottomans joined forces with Germany. This gave the British an excuse to invade Mesopotamia, which they did in November 1914. By 1918, Mesopotamia was under total British control.

After World War I ended, the League of Nations was formed in an attempt to guarantee world peace. In 1920, the League

British troops enter Baghdad in 1917. The British gained control of what is now Iraq following World War I.

of Nations gave the British a mandate to supervise the governing of the newly created state of Iraq. The British administrators of Iraq were disliked by the Iraqi people, who wanted total independence. The British decided to make Iraq a monarchy. They chose Faisal ibn Hussein, a member of the Hashemite Dynasty of Arabia, as the first monarch. Essentially, the British selected Faisal because the dynasty had supported the British against the Ottomans during World War I.

The final boundaries for Iraq were determined in 1925. The Europeans who set the new boundaries paid little attention to where different tribal and ethnic groups traditionally lived. The result was the creation of a state that would be constantly plagued by revolts and regular changes of leadership.

Fourteen-year-old King Faisal II of Iraq walks with his cousin Amir Abd al-Ilah in 1949. Abd al-Ilah served as regent until Faisal turned eighteen.

Independence

King Faisal ruled Iraq from 1921 until his death in 1933. He lived long enough to witness Iraq's independence on October 3, 1932. He was succeeded by his son, Ghazi, who died in an automobile accident in 1939. King Ghazi's son, Faisal II, became king at the age of three. The power of the monarchy rested in the hands of his first cousin, Abd al-Ilah, until Faisal grew up. Abd al-Ilah was pro-British and was frequently criticized by nationalist groups within Iraq. In general, the political system created by the British was not strong enough to allow for the peaceful transition of power. As a result, the Iraqi armed forces gained considerable political power. In 1958, a military coup toppled the monarchy and the old regime; both Abd al-Ilah and Faisal II were killed.

The Rise of the Ba'th Political Party

Abd al-Karim Qasim, one of the military leaders involved in the coup, became prime minister of Iraq. But Qasim's rule was largely ineffective because there were so many opposing groups. Members of one of these groups, the Ba'th Party, attempted to kill Qasim in 1959. Although Qasim was injured, he survived and brought seventy-eight Ba'thists to trial. One notable member of the assassination team escaped to Syria and then Egypt. His name was Saddam Hussein, and his survival would greatly alter Iraq's future.

In 1963, the Ba'th Party led a coup against Qasim. This time, Qasim was arrested and executed. The Ba'th Party came briefly to power and ruled alongside Arab nationalists under the presidency of Abd al-Salem Arif. In 1966, Arif was killed in a helicopter crash, and in 1968, the Ba'th came to power again, this time for good. For the next few years, coups, rebellions, and assassinations were common. On July 16, 1979, Hussein became president.

The Saddam Hussein Era

In some ways, Saddam Hussein proved to be an effective leader. As president, he used oil revenue to help Iraqi citizens

with massive projects that improved education, medical, and transportation facilities. But he also created a totalitarian state, ruthlessly eliminating any opposition. To consolidate his power, he established a strong internal security force to spy on Iraq's citizens. He also handed out political favors to the mostly Sunni members of his Ba'th Party.

Saddam Hussein (right) joined the Ba'th Party at age twenty and quickly became a leading member. After the Ba'thists came to power in 1968, he was appointed vice president of Iraq.

Hussein's regime was marked by three costly wars. The first was the Iran-Iraq War. In September 1980, fearing the intentions of the newly established Islamic Republic of Iran, Iraq's military forces invaded Iran. The conflict continued until 1988, killing hundreds of thousands of people in both Iraq and Iran and nearly bankrupting both nations. Finally, a formal ceasefire was negotiated. After the war, it was found that Hussein's troops had used chemical weapons against Iraq's own Kurdish citizens, who were agitating for independence. This raised suspicion about the level of Iraq's development of chemical and biological weapons. The United States had supported Iraq in its war against Iran, so few steps were taken against Iraq at that time.

The Gulf War

Saddam Hussein started a second costly war on August 2, 1990, when Iraqi military forces invaded Kuwait. Hussein justified

British troops head toward Iraq in 1990 in preparation for the Persian Gulf War. More than 40,000 British troops took part in the war.

the invasion by claiming that Kuwait was historically part of Basra Province. He also accused the Kuwaitis of overproducing oil and thus damaging Iraq's economy. Finally, Hussein claimed that the invasion was necessary to halt Kuwait's illegal pumping of oil from Iraq's Rumaila oil field, which straddles the border between the two nations.

The invasion proved disastrous for Iraq. The United Nations, an organization of nations around the world that works to keep peace, immediately passed a resolution calling for Iraq's withdrawal from Kuwait. When Iraq refused to leave, the United States organized a coalition military force from thirty-nine nations, which forced Iraq from Kuwait in the Gulf War. The coalition troops began bombing Iraq in January 1991. By February 27, 1991, Iraq was defeated. Before withdrawing, however, Hussein's troops set fire to most of Kuwait's oil wells, creating an environmental disaster in the region.

International economic sanctions against Iraq had also been put in place following the invasion of Kuwait. In most cases, nations were not supposed to trade with Iraq except for food and medicine. These sanctions were strongly enforced between 1990 and 2003.

The Iraq War

The September 11, 2001, attack by al-Qaeda terrorists on the United States raised questions about Saddam Hussein's participation in world terrorism. President George W. Bush accused Hussein of being an al-Qaeda supporter and of developing weapons of mass destruction. On March 17, 2003, Bush demanded that Hussein leave the country within forty-eight hours, or the United States would pursue military action against Iraq. Hussein ignored Bush's threat, and on March 19, 2003, U.S. troops and other coalition forces entered Iraq. On May 1, 2003, Bush declared that the Iraq War had ended. Hussein had been forced from power, but no weapons of mass destruction were found and no ties to al-Qaeda were proven. Violence continued on a daily basis after the war's official end, as a result of the opposition by various groups to the American presence there.

Young Iraqis are accustomed to seeing military vehicles on the street.

The war and thirteen years of economic sanctions largely destroyed the infrastructure of Iraq. But the country had entered a new era, with a fragile democracy supported by U.S. military forces and some coalition troops. The Iraqi people have suffered greatly, but they cling to a thin thread of hope that the future will be brighter.

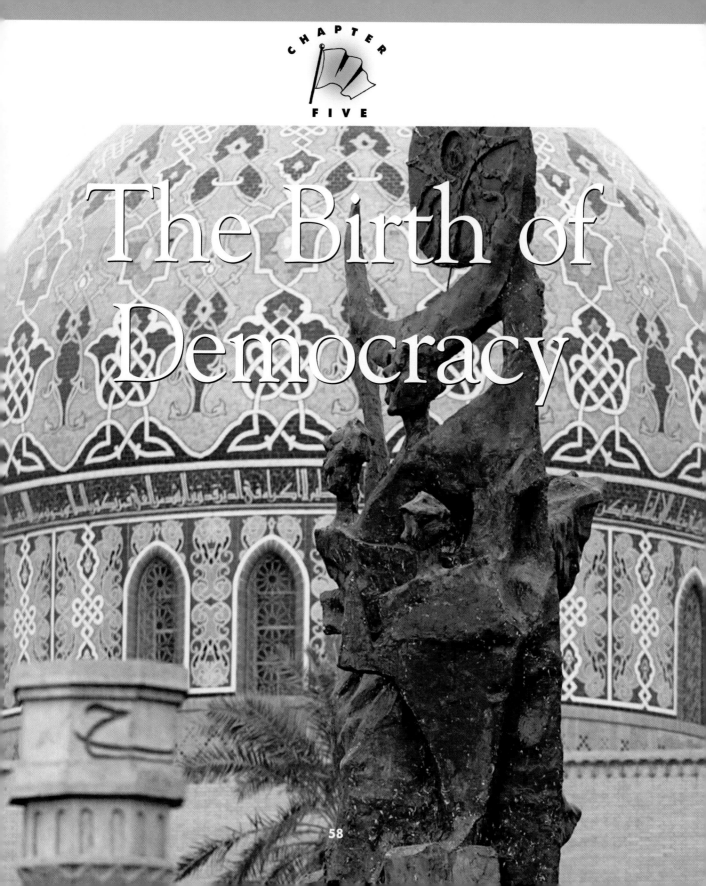

The Birth of Democracy

THE MODERN STATE OF IRAQ IS A RELATIVELY RECENT creation. The country was carved out of the remnants of the Ottoman Empire following World War I. Outsiders, particularly the British and French, determined the national boundaries. In the process of establishing several new countries in the Middle East, these European powers paid little attention to cultural traditions of the area. As a result, they created a nation that would be extremely difficult to govern. In Iraq, there are three distinct cultural groups. The Shi'i Muslims dominate in the south. The Sunni Muslims are most significant in central Iraq, and the Kurds hold the majority in the north.

Opposite: **A statue of Saddam Hussein that stood on a pedestal in Baghdad's al-Firdos Square was knocked down after he was overthrown. In May 2003, a group of artists put their own statue on the pedestal.**

The Flag of Iraq

The flag of Iraq has three equal horizontal bands of red, white, and black. In the middle white band, there are three green five-pointed stars and the words *Allahu Akbar*, which mean "God is great" in Arabic. This phrase was added to the flag in 1991 at the beginning of the Gulf War.

Red, white, black, and green are symbols of Pan-Arabism, or Arab unity. The three green stars originally represented Iraq, Egypt, and Syria, which at one point planned to form a single political union. Today, the three stars represent the Ba'th Party's motto, "Unity, Freedom, and Socialism." Because the Ba'th Party is no longer in power, it is likely that the new government of Iraq will adopt a new flag.

Monarchy and Dictatorship

Although Iraq gained formal independence in 1932, Iraqi citizens had little input in their government. The British had controlled Iraq following World War I. Their occupation was unpopular, so they tried to ease the dissent by creating a monarchy. In 1921, they selected Faisal, a non-Iraqi Arab from Mecca, Arabia, to rule the country. The monarchy lasted until 1958, but it was never popular with the Iraqi people, who felt that the British were still making most of the decisions.

From 1958 to 1968, the government was controlled by military officers who had come to power by overthrowing the monarchy. At first, they were popular because they cut ties with the British. But their popularity faded rapidly, and they were replaced by Ba'th Party members in 1968.

From 1968 to 2003 the Ba'th Party governed Iraq. The Ba'athists advocated the spread of Arab unity across the Middle East. The party's most notable leader, Saddam Hussein, took over the presidency in 1979 and led Iraq for twenty-four years. All major decisions regarding the governing of Iraq were in his hands. In 2003, a coalition military force led by U.S. and British troops toppled Hussein's regime. This began a new phase in how Iraq's citizens would be governed.

Saddam Hussein (right) was a ruthless dictator, but he was popular with some Arabs because he stood up to the West.

Saddam Hussein

Saddam Hussein, the former president and dictator of Iraq, was born into poverty in the village of al-Awja near Tikrit in 1936. He took an early interest in politics at the urging of an uncle. He joined the Ba'th Party because of the party's support of Arab nationalism. Hussein was involved in a Ba'th Party attempt to kill Abd al-Karim Qasim, Iraq's new military leader, in 1959. Hussein was wounded in the attempt and fled to Egypt, where he finished his high school education.

When he returned to Iraq in 1963, he immediately became involved in Ba'th Party politics. His outspoken nature led to his arrest and a two-year prison term. Upon his release, he rapidly worked his way to the number-two position in the Ba'th Party, which by then controlled Iraq. In July 1979, he became president. He maintained an iron grip on the country until his ouster by outside military forces led by the United States and the United Kingdom in 2003.

During his time in office, oil revenue increased substantially. Hussein used the new money to improve education, transportation, housing, and a public health system. He also spent large amounts of oil wealth to build a strong military and internal security service, to encourage research in chemical weapons, and to build elaborate palaces for himself.

Hussein's major legacy is his decisions that involved Iraq in three disastrous wars. These conflicts bankrupted the Iraqi economy and ruined Iraq's infrastructure. He is also remembered for his brutal treatment of anyone who opposed his policies. He killed many of his own citizens including an estimated seventy thousand Kurds in 1988 and twenty thousand Shi'is in 1991.

The Path to Democracy

In May 2003, President George W. Bush announced the end of the Iraq War. Coalition military forces led by U.S. and British troops prepared to occupy Iraq while a new government was formed. A temporary administrative organization called the Coalition Provisional Authority (CPA) was established. The CPA was charged with preparing Iraqis to govern themselves and rebuild the war-torn nation.

When President George W. Bush announced the end of major combat in the Iraq War on May 1, 2003, 137 American troops had been killed in the fighting. By October 2005, the number of American military deaths had risen to 2,000.

The first step in the process was the creation of a twenty-five-member Iraqi Governing Council. The council generally reflected population percentages of ethnic and religious groups in Iraq. There were thirteen Shi'i Muslims, five Sunni Muslims, five Kurds, one Assyrian Christian, and one Turkman on the council. They had the power to appoint government ministers and diplomatic representatives.

On June 30, 2004, the CPA ceased to exist and an interim government took over. Iraqis were now governing their own country, though security issues were primarily in the hands of foreign occupation troops.

The interim government served for seven months. It administered Iraqi political affairs and, when the security situation permitted, conducted normal business in the best interests of its citizens. Its primary responsibility was to prepare the country for national elections on January 30, 2005. These elections would determine the formation of a transitional government, the final step before the establishment of a permanent Iraqi government.

The Elections

Many political analysts did not believe that fair elections could be safely conducted in Iraq in 2005. But more than eight million Iraqi citizens (58 percent of registered voters) cast their ballots. They elected 275 members to the Iraqi National Assembly. Assembly members then selected administrative officials to lead the executive branch of the Iraqi transitional government.

Voter turnout was especially heavy in Kurdish areas in the north and Shi'i districts in the south. Sunni Arabs, who had composed the major part of Saddam Hussein's government, gained only a few legislative seats in the Iraqi National Assembly. Many Sunnis did not participate because they felt fair elections were impossible or feared violence if they took part.

Women were active in the election process. Eighty-five women were elected to the Iraqi National Assembly, and six women were appointed as cabinet ministers. Many of the elected female assembly members are Shi'i with distinctly conservative views.

It was a proud moment for many Iraqis when they voted for the members of Iraq's transitional government in January 2005.

The Iraqi transitional government was charged with drafting a new constitution. Prime Minister Ibrahim al-Jafari had the responsibility of leading the transitional government through this difficult task. He is a prominent Shi'i Muslim who opposed Hussein's regime and fled to the United Kingdom to avoid torture and death.

A Permanent Government

Drafting a new constitution for Iraq was difficult. Three powerful groups—Kurds, Shi'is, and Sunnis—had to agree on a final draft, and they all had very different agendas. The Kurds wanted more autonomy in the north. The Shi'is, who make up roughly 60 percent of the population, wanted the power that

Prior to the American-led invasion of Iraq, Ibrahim al-Jafari had lived in London, England, for fourteen years. From there, he worked to organize opposition to Saddam Hussein's rule.

customarily goes to a nation's majority group. The Sunnis, who controlled the country for many years as the principal members of the Ba'th Party, did not want to give up their position of strength. In October 2005, Iraqi voters approved a new constitution.

The biggest challenge to the establishment of a permanent, democratically elected government is security. No government can survive if it cannot provide security to its citizens. In the aftermath of Hussein's ouster, Iraq suffered frequent assassinations, suicide bombings, and other violent crimes. In the first eighteen months alone after President Bush declared the Iraq War over, such violence killed more than twelve thousand people, mostly Iraqi civilians. To establish a permanent government, Iraq's new army and coalition forces will have to end this chaos. It will require courage and determination, and it will likely take many years before peace and stability are restored.

In the aftermath of the Iraq War, violence was rampant. The streets of Baghdad, a city of more than five million, were sometimes empty as people stayed inside out of fear.

Baghdad: Did You Know This?

The city of Baghdad was founded in A.D. 762 by Abu Ja'far al-Mansur, caliph of the Abbasid Dynasty. Baghdad is located along the banks of the Tigris River at an elevation of 112 feet (34 m) above sea level. The average January temperature is 48°F (8.9°C), and the average July temperature is 94°F (34.4°C). In most years, Baghdad receives an average of only 6 inches (15 cm) of rain. The summers are extremely dry, with little or no rain falling from June through September. In 2002, Baghdad had an estimated population of 5,605,000.

Baghdad is Iraq's capital and its major center of manufacturing. It is home to many important museums, archaeological sites, mosques, and government buildings, including the Iraq Museum and the Abbasid Palace. The city was badly damaged by bombings and missile attacks in the Gulf War and the Iraq War. Several years and large investments of money and labor will be necessary to rebuild Baghdad.

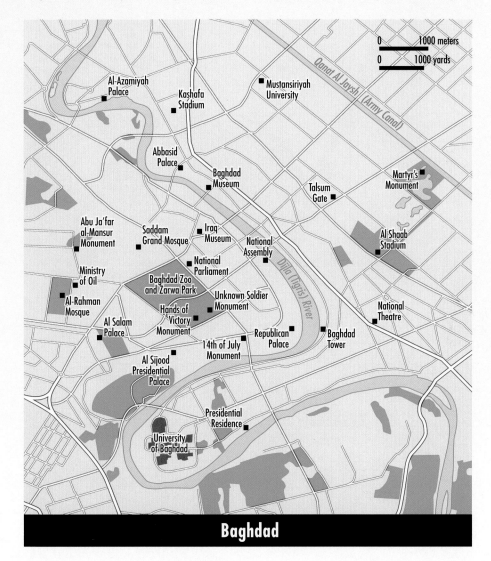

Baghdad

Black Gold

FOR MUCH OF THE LAST CENTURY, IRAQ'S ECONOMY HAS BEEN driven by one thing: oil. The history of oil in Iraq is filled with intrigue, colonialism, imperialism, fraud, broken promises, and unimagined wealth.

Oil is Iraq's number-one product.

Oil: A Blessing and a Curse

The story opens with the discovery of oil in neighboring Iran in 1908. Immediately, world attention became focused on the Middle East as a potential new source of oil. Some Western geologists claimed to be archaeologists studying Iraq's ancient civilizations so they could visit the country and investigate the likelihood of oil reserves. They did not leave Iraq disappointed. They saw oil oozing from surface cracks and smelled the foul odor of sulfur gas, and they knew oil was there.

After oil was discovered at Masjed Soleyman in Iran in 1908, geologists rushed into Iraq in search of oil.

During World War I, the British moved quickly to establish a military presence in Iraq. Following the war, they were given control of Iraq. The British had an increasing thirst for oil to fuel their navy, and they hoped that Iraqi oil would quench that thirst.

Prior to British occupation, Western oil companies were already preparing to exploit Iraqi oil. The Turkish Petroleum Company (TPC) was founded in 1912. It was renamed the Iraq Petroleum Company (IPC) in 1929. British companies controlled almost half of the TPC. French and American companies controlled most of the rest. In 1927, the TPC signed an oil agreement with Iraq and prepared to begin drilling. Western oil companies were now in control of Iraq's oil and would be until 1972.

The oil business in Iraq has had its ups and downs because of war. This 1932 photo shows the oil business during its early prosperous time.

A Thundering Roar

In October 1927, the TPC began to drill its first well in the 60-mile (100 km) long Kirkuk geologic structure. After a few days of drilling, the ground began to tremble and the drilling rig started shaking violently. Suddenly, oil and gas erupted up from the well like lava from a volcano. The drillers lost control of the well as oil shot 50 feet (15 m) into the air. During the next nine days, almost 4 million gallons (15 million liters) of crude oil would drench the surrounding area before the well was controlled. The gusher, named Baba Gurgur I, claimed two lives and introduced the world to Iraq's oil wealth.

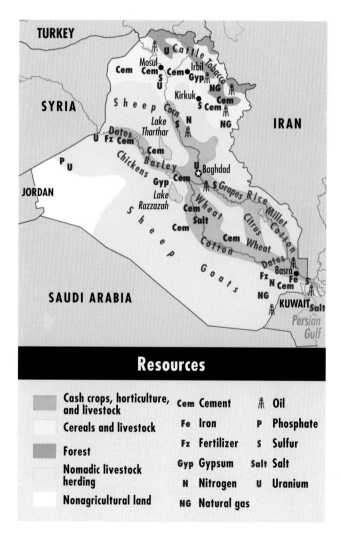

The IPC continued to explore for oil. In 1949, it discovered the Zubair field. The huge Rumaila reserves were discovered in 1953. Soon, the Bai Hassan field and the Jambur reserves had also been found. In 1961, the government passed a law that turned drilling rights over the unexploited parts of Iraq to the Iraqi National Oil Company. In 1972, the entire oil industry was nationalized, and finally the Iraqi people owned their oil resources. By 1979, Iraq was producing 3.5 million barrels of oil a day.

War and sabotage have wreaked havoc on Iraq's oil industry. In 2005, Iraq's oil production dropped to its lowest level in a decade.

Saddam Hussein and Oil

The oil industry provided great wealth to Saddam Hussein's government. Unfortunately, he squandered much of the oil income on wars and his own personal excesses. The oil industry was seriously damaged by the Iran-Iraq War of the 1980s and the Gulf War of 1991. Additional damage resulted from economic sanctions and the Iraq War that led to the removal of Hussein.

The Current Picture

Iraq is believed to have the world's second-largest oil reserves. Current proven oil reserves are around 112 billion barrels. Most geologists are confident that the reserves will exceed 200 billion barrels. Western Iraq is largely unexplored, and the potential for development is immense.

Besides Iraq's large supply of oil, two other factors make it appealing to oil companies. The first is the quality of Iraq's oil. It has high carbon content and low sulfur content. The other factor is that most of Iraq's oil is located at shallow depths. More than one-third of the reserves are within 1,800 feet (550 m) of the surface. This lowers production costs to $1.50 per barrel compared with $20.00 per barrel for deep wells.

There is little doubt that Iraqi oil could fuel an economic rebirth for the nation. Before that can occur, however, aging and war-damaged equipment will have to be replaced. Security must be improved at oil fields, refineries, and along pipelines. Finally, the question of who will rebuild and pay for the cost of reconstruction must be answered.

What Iraq Grows, Makes, and Mines

Agriculture (2002)

Wheat	1,000,000 metric tons
Dates	650,000 metric tons
Barley	500,000 metric tons

Manufacturing (2004)

Petroleum refining	150 million barrels
Cement	2,040,000 metric tons
Phosphate products	50,000 metric tons

Mining (2002)

Petroleum	740 million barrels
Natural gas	7 billion cubic meters
Salt	300,000 metric tons

Other Minerals

Iraq is also a world leader in natural gas reserves, with an estimated 110 trillion cubic feet (31,150,000,000 cubic meters) of gas. Most of the natural gas is trapped above oil layers in the major oil fields. Much of the gas is used to generate electricity in Iraq.

Iraq produces minor amounts of sulfur, phosphate, and gypsum. Limestone, which is found in many regions of the country, is used in the cement industry.

Growing the Country's Food

Agriculture has been an important part of this region's economy since the Sumerians first began irrigating crops more than five thousand years ago. Today, agriculture remains important, employing almost 20 percent of the people. Wheat, dates, barley, and rice lead the list of crops produced in Iraq. Livestock production is dominated by sheep, goats, and cattle. There are three distinct regions of agriculture in Iraq.

The largest block of agricultural land is found in northeastern Iraq, one of the few regions of the country that is not arid. The region gets enough precipitation during the winter to produce cereal crops like wheat and barley. Sheep and goats are grazed on the slopes of the mountains. Some fruit and vegetables are also grown. These crops are often irrigated from the streams that flow down the mountains.

Irrigated fields have dominated the landscape along the floodplains of the Tigris and the Euphrates rivers for thousands of years. The flooding rivers have repeatedly deposited rich layers

of silt across the floodplains. Water from the rivers gives life to plants that could otherwise not exist in the desert environment. A variety of crops are grown in the land between the rivers, but date palms, rice, vegetables, and wheat dominate. A limited amount of cotton is grown to supply the textile industry.

Most of the land located west of the Euphrates River and the upper Tigris River basin is unsuitable for crops. It is a true desert with poor soil. Some sheep and goats are grazed over huge expanses of land because the plant life is so limited.

Sheep are Iraq's most common livestock. It is estimated that there are about five million sheep in northern Iraq alone.

New Money

In October 2003, the Central Bank of Iraq released the new Iraqi dinar as the country's legal currency. Paper banknotes include 50, 250, 500, 1,000, 5,000, 10,000, and 25,000 dinar notes. In January 2005, three coins with values of 25, 50, and 100 dinars were introduced. In 2005, 1 U.S. dollar equaled 1,470 dinars.

Problems on the Horizon

The Ataturk Dam on the Euphrates River provides people in Turkey with electricity and irrigation water, but it reduces the flow of water downstream in Iraq.

At one time, Iraq could feed its citizens without importing much additional food. Today, the nation imports more than half its food needs. Agriculture, like other sectors of the economy, has been devastated by the recent wars. Irrigation canals and drainage canals have been damaged and destroyed. Pumping equipment, tractors, fertilizer supplies, and livestock medicines have been unavailable because of economic sanctions or damaged ports and highways.

Iraq's agriculture also faces major problems having to do with water. Both the Tigris and Euphrates rivers begin in Turkey. Turkey is building mammoth dams on both rivers, and Syria has constructed a large dam on the Euphrates. It is entirely possible that Iraq could lose half of its water supply in the next few years. The problem is not only the quantity of water but also the quality. As the volume of water decreases, the salt content increases. The increase in the amount of salt in the water could poison the soil, so that crops will not grow.

Manufacturing

Industry has always been a weak link in the Iraqi economy. During the British period of influence, Iraq was encouraged to buy manufactured products from the United Kingdom. After the Ba'th Party came to power, most production came from government-owned factories that did not function well. In recent years, wars and international economic sanctions limited Iraqi access to raw materials and machinery. Trade has been hindered by damaged transportation and communications networks. Today, Iraq produces modest amounts of cement, processed food, textiles, leather, fertilizer, beverages, and paper products, but few Iraqi products are exported.

Iraq has few factories. In 2005, there were just thirty-one textile plants in the entire country.

The Dawra oil refinery was built in the 1950s. The facility, which is badly in need of repair and updating, supplies about half of Baghdad's oil.

It is not surprising that in a nation with huge oil reserves, petroleum refining is the major industry. There are eight oil refineries in Iraq. The three largest are located at Baiji in the north, Basra in the south, and the Dawra complex near Baghdad. The refineries are connected to a national network of pipelines that carry the oil from major producing fields. Although the refineries can handle 415,000 barrels per day, production is less than one-third of that.

Iraq's refining industry is plagued by three major problems. The first is the physical condition of the refineries. The equipment is old, worn out, or damaged from military action. If the refineries are not updated, accidents and environmental damage will be a constant threat.

Second, the pipelines, pumping stations, and refineries themselves are regular victims of sabotage by people opposed to the Iraqis in power and to the U.S. presence there. Attacks on the refining industry have reduced production by more than half. Despite all its oil, Iraq has to import large quantities of gasoline to meet its citizens' needs.

Looting presents a third problem. Thieves sometimes drill into pipelines and steal crude oil or refined products to sell. Their action frequently results in major leaks, which harm the environment.

Improving Industry

Iraq has the labor force and raw materials to greatly improve the industrial sector of its economy. Industrial growth, however, will not occur until the roads, ports, railways, electrical plants, pipelines, and other infrastructure that have been damaged in recent wars are repaired. Restoring these services will cost huge amounts of money, take a great deal of time, and require major improvements in security across the nation.

Workers repair a pipeline near Basra following an attack. In the years after Saddam Hussein was ousted, there were an average of three attacks a week on Iraqi oil equipment.

A Diverse
Population

I RAQ'S POPULATION REACHED
approximately 26 million in 2005.
Iraq has a young population, with
more than 40 percent of its people under fourteen years old, and
it is growing quickly. This population is quite diverse. The nation has
two major ethnic groups and several
minority populations. Iraq is offi-
cially bilingual, with both Arabic
and Kurdish being official languages,
but other languages can be heard in
different areas of the country.

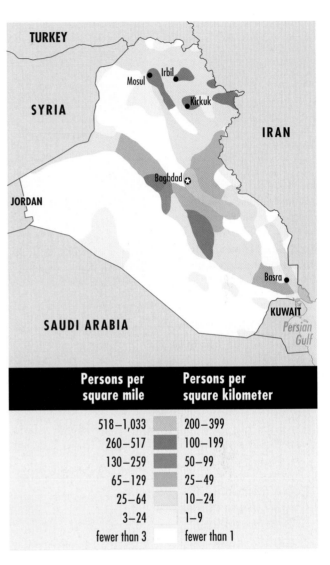

Persons per square mile		Persons per square kilometer
518–1,033		200–399
260–517		100–199
130–259		50–99
65–129		25–49
25–64		10–24
3–24		1–9
fewer than 3		fewer than 1

Where Do People Live?

Nature plays a huge role in where
people live in Iraq. Almost 40 percent
of the land in Iraq has an extremely
low population density. These are
the desert regions of western and
southwestern Iraq, which simply will not support many
people. The northeast, which receives adequate rainfall,
supports much greater population densities. There are also
large concentrations of people in the dry areas of southeastern Iraq. In this region, waters from the Tigris and

Opposite: **Marsh Arabs traditionally lived in the marshy
areas of southern Iraq. In
1991, 250,000 Marsh Arabs
lived there, but today that
number is probably closer to
20,000.**

In the last half of the twentieth century, the Iraqi countryside emptied rapidly. In 1947, 61 percent of Iraqis lived in rural areas. That number had dropped to 33 percent by 2003.

Who Lives in Iraq?

Arabs	75–80%
Kurds	15–20%
Others (Turkmen, Assyrians, etc.)	3%

Population of Iraq's Largest Cities (2002 estimates)

Baghdad	5,605,000
Mosul	1,739,000
Basra	1,337,000
Irbil	839,000
Kirkuk	728,000
Sulaymaniyah	643,000
Najaf	563,000

the Euphrates rivers support irrigation, so larger population densities can thrive.

On the Move

Over the past thirty years, one of the major changes Iraq has seen is the move of people from rural areas to cities. The countryside is emptying. Today, two-thirds of all Iraqis live in cities. Baghdad, Mosul, and Basra all have populations of more than one million. Baghdad, which is home to 5,605,000 people, is rapidly becoming one of the largest cities in the Middle East.

People move to the cities for many reasons. Farmers are tired of bad weather conditions and low prices for their products. People tire of living in poverty in small houses, struggling to survive. They believe that cities offer better opportunities for health care, jobs, and education. The flow of rural citizens into the urban areas is likely to continue.

Words of Wisdom

Arab Proverbs

"A sharp tongue cuts deeper than a sword."

"The giver of charity should not mention it; and the receiver should not forget it."

"If you are a frequent liar, you had better have a good memory."

Kurdish Proverbs

"A fool dreams of wealth, a wise man of happiness."

"A thousand friends are too few; one enemy is too many."

"Beauty passes, wisdom remains."

Ethnic Diversity

Sometimes ethnic diversity can enrich the social fabric of a nation. Other times, it can help destroy the foundations of a society. In Iraq, ethnic diversity has resulted in power struggles, the brutal treatment of minorities, and an ever-increasing mistrust and misunderstanding between groups.

The Arabs

The Arabs swept into present-day Iraq from the Arabian Peninsula beginning in 633. They soon conquered the region. Today, Arabs make up 75 to 80 percent of Iraq's total population. The Arabs brought two major cultural identities with them: their language (Arabic) and their religion (Islam).

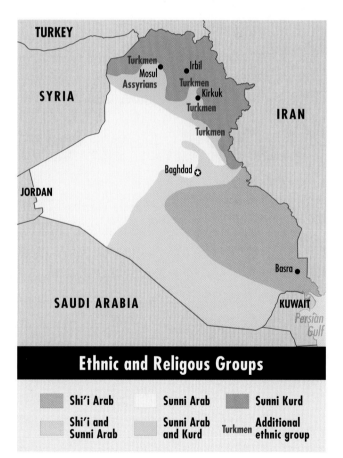

Ethnic and Religous Groups

- Shi'i Arab
- Shi'i and Sunni Arab
- Sunni Arab
- Sunni Arab and Kurd
- Sunni Kurd
- Turkmen Additional ethnic group

Sunni Arab protesters carry a picture of Saddam Hussein. Many Sunnis believe that they will have little political power in the new Iraq.

The Arabic language and the Muslim religion dominate Iraq. While Iraqi Arabs have many things in common, one major difference among them has prevented the Arabs from being unified. That difference is actually religion.

About 60 percent of Iraq's Arab population are followers of the Shi'i sect of Islam. The Shi'i primarily live in southern Iraq, particularly in the southeast.

The Ma'dan are frequently referred to as the Marsh Arabs. They are Shi'i Muslims whose ancestors have lived in the reed marshes of the lower Tigris-Euphrates river valley for more than five thousand years. After the 1991 Gulf War, Saddam Hussein killed thousands of Ma'dan and drove most of the survivors into exile in Iran.

The Sunni Arabs account for some 20 percent of Iraq's population. They live in central and northern Iraq, with heavy concentrations in Baghdad and Tikrit. Saddam Hussein and most leading members of the Ba'th Party were Sunni Arabs. They dominated the politics and economy of Iraq from 1968 until Hussein's ouster in 2003.

The Kurds

It is estimated that 5 million Kurds live in Iraq. The Kurds of Iraq are part of a larger Kurdish population that spreads across a vast area known as Kurdistan. This region includes parts of Turkey, Iran, Iraq, and Syria. The Kurds were promised independence after World War I, but that promise was broken. In Iraq, most Kurds live in the northeastern corner of the country. They have been largely self-governing since the creation of a "safe haven" by the United States and the United Kingdom in April 1991, after the Gulf War.

Most of the world's 25 million Kurds live in a swath of mountainous land that stretches across Syria, Turkey, Iraq, and Iran. The Kurds are thought to be the world's largest ethnic group without their own country.

Kurdish society is still strongly tribal, and many of those who have not moved to cities maintain allegiances to tribal chiefs rather than a central government. Many Kurds are excellent horsemen and accomplished soldiers. Most are Sunni Muslims. They tend to be fairly liberal and generally provide women with greater opportunities than Arab Iraqis do. Kurds have their own language, Kurdish, which is closely related to Persian, the language of Iran.

The Turkmen

The Turkmen, the third-largest ethnic group in Iraq, make up about 2 percent of the population. Their ancestors came from central Asia and settled in Iraq thousands of years ago. The Turkmen and the Kurds share the same area in northeastern Iraq. Many Turkmen live in the cities of Irbil and Kirkuk. Most are Sunni Muslims who speak a Turkish dialect.

Many Turkmen feel that the new Iraqi government has ignored them in favor of the Kurds. They have strong ties with the government of Turkey, which historically has been anti-Kurdish. If the Turkish government feels that the Turkmen in Iraq are being treated unfairly, especially by the Kurds, it could contribute to instability in the region.

Kirkuk is home to most of the Turkmen of Iraq. It is a diverse city, with large communities of Turkmen, Kurds, Assyrians, and Arabs.

Assyrian Christians attend a service in Mosul.

Assyrians and Armenians

The Assyrians are descendants of one of the oldest and most powerful civilizations ever established in Mesopotamia. The Assyrians have sometimes been persecuted or massacred. Many of the Assyrians now living in Iraq fled persecution in Turkey.

Most Assyrians live in northwestern Iraq, especially the city of Mosul. They can also be found working as professionals and businesspeople in most large cities. Assyrians are one of the few original Christian groups that still survive in the Middle East. Their spoken language is a dialect of Aramaic, the language of much of the region at the time of Jesus.

Armenians are an ethnic group originally from a region north of Iraq. They have lived in Iraq for centuries. Together, there are about a million Armenian and Assyrian Christians in Iraq.

What's in a Name?

Kurdish Names and Meanings

Female Names	Male Names
Awaz—Music	Bakhtiar—Successful
Awat—Hope	Dilshad—A happy heart
Dilsoz—Honest	Milar—King
Kazhal—Beautiful	Nichivan—Hunter
Shirin—Sweet	Rzgar—A free man

Arab Names and Meanings

Female Names	Male Names
Jamila—Beautiful	Abd-allah—Servant of God
Karima—Generous	Hakim—Wise
Nabila—Noble	Jamil—Handsome
Najeeba—Smart, intelligent	Nabil—Noble
Sharifa—Honest, trustworthy	Nasser—Liberator

Arabic is written in a beautiful flowing script that reads from right to left.

Iraq has two official languages: Arabic and Kurdish. Arabic is spoken as a first language by 75 to 80 percent of the population. Arabic is a member of the Semitic family of languages, which also includes Hebrew and Aramaic. The Arabic alphabet has twenty-eight letters. Arabic is written from right to left, the opposite of how English is written. Many English words are derived from Arabic, including *admiral*, *algebra*, *almanac*, *coffee*, *cotton*, and *giraffe*.

Kurdish is most often heard in northeastern Iraq. Interestingly, there is not a standard alphabet for Kurdish. Kurds educated in Turkey use the Roman alphabet. Other Kurds use the Cyrillic alphabet, which is used in Russia. The Kurds of Iraq use the Arabic alphabet, but they have added some letters to the alphabet to represent Kurdish sounds that do not exist in Arabic.

The Kurds have their own language. Some Kurds can speak Arabic, but few Arabs speak Kurdish.

Common Words and Phrases

English	Iraqi Arabic	Kurdish
What is your name?	Shu ismak?	Navê te çi ye?
Hello	Marhaba	Çawan î
Good-bye	Ma' assalama	Bi xêr biçî
Please	Minfadlik	Bê zeĥ met
Thank you	Shukran	Memnun

The recent wars in Iraq destroyed school property and left the country with little money to pay teachers or buy supplies. In 2003, only one in six Iraqi children had textbooks.

Back to School

Prior to the start of the Iran-Iraq War in 1980, Iraq had some of the best-educated citizens in the Middle East. Its high literacy rate was the envy of many neighboring countries. Six years of education were required of all children. The government paid for all educational costs from elementary school through college. Thousands of new schools had been built.

Over the past twenty-five years, however, war, economic sanctions, and a bankrupt economy have badly damaged the educational system. Literacy rates for the youth of Iraq have dropped alarmingly, to 40 or 50 percent. Schools are overcrowded. Desks, books, and teaching materials are in short supply. Teachers are poorly trained and teach mostly by using memorization. The exchange of ideas and development of critical-thinking skills have always been rare in Iraq's classrooms. Many children drop out of school. Some quit to work because their family needs the income. Others fear violence.

Despite the upheaval in Iraqi in recent years, many university classrooms are full. By and large, college campuses have been a safe haven for students and have seen little violence. College students are allowed to enter into debate with their professors. Some professors are concerned that students are primarily interested in discussing politics and religion at the expense of their other subjects.

No country can build a strong economy without a sound educational system. For Iraq to achieve this, it will require a unified effort by all ethnic and religious groups. Security must be provided for the safety of schoolchildren. In the absence of a safe environment for learning, the future will be bleak.

The University of Baghdad is the largest university in Iraq, with as many as forty thousand students.

A Muslim Nation

ISLAM SPREAD RAPIDLY FROM ITS BIRTHPLACE IN MECCA, in what is now Saudi Arabia, after the death of Muhammad in 632. Within one hundred years of Muhammad's death, devout Muslims had carried the new religion across North Africa and deep into Europe. Most people living on the Arabian Peninsula converted to Islam. As the Muslim conquest continued, it swept into Pakistan and across northern India. Converts accepted the faith in central Asia and western China. In one century, Islam had claimed hundreds of thousands of new followers. Most people living in what is now Iraq had converted to Islam by the early eleventh century.

Opposite: **About 97 percent of Iraqis are Muslim.**

Religions of Iraq

Shi'i Muslim	60–65%
Sunni Muslim	32–37%
Christian	3%

Muslims are required to pray five times a day.

The Prophet Muhammad

Muhammad was born in Mecca, Arabia, in 570. He was from a family of successful merchants, and he himself was a skilled businessperson who earned a reputation as an honest merchant.

Mecca was a prosperous city. Its citizens were pagans who worshipped idols. This behavior offended Muhammad. Because he was a serious man, he often entered a cave on Mount Hira, near Mecca, to pray and meditate. According to Muslim belief, at forty years old Muhammad began receiving revelations from the archangel Gabriel. These revelations became the Qur'an, the holy book of Islam.

Muhammad then began to teach the principles of the Qur'an in Mecca. His teachings irritated the Meccans. They hatched a plan to kill him, but he escaped and fled to Medina. Muhammad's escape occurred in 622 and is called the *Hijira*.

The people of Medina accepted Muhammad's teachings. After three major battles with the Meccans, Muhammad and his followers returned to Mecca and took control of the city in 630. Mecca became the most important city of the new religion of Islam. Today, more than 1.2 billion Muslims worldwide accept the teachings of the Prophet Muhammad.

A young girl prays at the shrine to Hussein, Muhammad's grandson, who is one of the most revered figures for Shi'i Muslims. More than 15 million Iraqis are Shi'i.

The Fire of Faith

Why did this new religion spread so rapidly? Historians have several explanations. First, the Muslim armies were able to conquer new areas quickly because these regions were already militarily exhausted. The Muslims who arrived were enthusiastic about sharing their beliefs. The concept of brotherhood and equality made the faith attractive to the new converts. Also, the simplicity of Islam was easy for largely uneducated converts to understand. Finally, both the military and the religious leadership of early Islam were of a very high quality.

The mosque is the Islamic place of worship. Muslims always face Mecca when they pray.

The Five Pillars

The beliefs of Sunni and Shi'i Muslims have some differences, but the similarities are much stronger. All Muslims are committed to following the definition of the word *Islam*, which means "submission to the will of God." In Iraq, the Arabic phrase "In'shallah" is used frequently at the end of a sentence, conveying the concept that if God is willing, it will happen. Muslims are guided by five major components of their religion. These are called the Five Pillars of Islam.

The *Shahadah* is the first pillar. It is a short statement that every Muslim makes when accepting the faith. Each true Muslim declares, "There is no god except God, and Muhammad is the Messenger of God." Once an individual makes this statement truthfully, in front of a witness, he becomes an accepted member of the religion.

The second pillar is *Salat*, or praying five times each day. The prayers, which follow a set pattern, are recited at precise times that are usually listed in local newspapers. In addition, Muslims are called to prayer from loudspeakers located high on the minaret (tower) of most mosques. The first prayer is offered at dawn, and others follow at noon, midafternoon, sunset, and nightfall.

Shi'i Muslims at Friday prayer in Baghdad. On Fridays, Muslims gather to pray in a group.

If possible, the prayers are recited in a mosque. But if a mosque is not available, the prayers can be said in factories, fields, schools, offices, at home, or other places. The prayers are always said in Arabic no matter what the native language of the speaker is. Muslims face Mecca when they say their prayers. Men and women seldom pray together, and if they do, they are separated by dividers.

The third pillar of Islam is *Sawm*, or fasting during the Islamic month of Ramadan. Ramadan is one of twelve months on the Islamic calendar and lasts twenty-nine or thirty days. During Ramadan, devout Muslims do not eat or drink from sunrise to sunset. They also try to refrain from having evil thoughts or desires during this period.

Sawm is supposed to remind Muslims that many people suffer daily from hunger and thirst. Fasting creates empathy and understanding for the difficulties of people living in poverty and need. Families spend a great deal of time together during Ramadan, so it helps build strong family relationships.

The fourth pillar of Islam is *Zakat*, or sharing the blessings that God provides each individual. This means that Muslims give money to help those in need. Each Muslim decides how much to give. Many Muslims dedicate about 2.5 percent of their income to Zakat. Donations can be given to less-fortunate people, to mosques, or to organizations like the Red Crescent Society, which is the Islamic equivalent of the International Red Cross.

The fifth and last pillar of Islam is *Hajj*. Hajj is a pilgrimage to Mecca that all Muslims are supposed to make during their

lives if they are able. For most Muslims, the pilgrimage is the most significant religious experience they will ever have. Some pilgrims save for their entire lives so that they can participate in this life-changing event. Two million Muslims from all over the world participate in the Hajj each year. Non-Muslims are not allowed to enter Mecca.

Muslim pilgrims travel to Mecca, Saudi Arabia, for the annual Hajj rituals. It is estimated over two million people attended this event in 2005.

The Qur'an says that people should dress modestly. In some communities, women wear long robes and head coverings when they leave their homes.

Living as a Muslim

Islam has many rules that guide everyday life. Muslims, like Jews, are not allowed to eat pork, because pigs are considered unclean animals. Alcohol is banned because it can harm human behavior and health. Muslims are not allowed to gamble because it involves making money at someone else's expense without working. Suicide is prohibited because taking one's own life is considered as serious an offense to God as murder.

Muslims also believe that women should only wear modest clothing. Religious statues, photos, or any other images are discouraged. Unlike many Christian churches that are filled with statues, crosses, and images of Jesus, Muslim mosques and homes are devoid of such objects.

Iraq's Muslims

Almost all Iraqis are followers of Islam. Some are extremely devout, while others are part-time Muslims or do not practice their religion. Religious issues are likely to play a large role in any new government in Iraq. The Shi'is, who were persecuted by Saddam Hussein's regime, are ready to claim political power as the majority.

The Tomb of Hussein

The city of Karbala contains the most important Shi'i religious shrine in the world. It is the tomb of Hussein ibn Ali Abu Talib. He was the grandson of the Prophet Muhammad and the son of Ali, the fourth caliph of Islam. He and more than seventy of his followers were murdered in 680 by troops of the Umayyad caliph of Damascus.

Shi'i Muslims make pilgrimages to Karbala twice each year. The first pilgrimage is on the tenth day of the Islamic month of Muharram, the date of Hussein's death. The second pilgrimage occurs forty days later at the end of the official mourning period marking his death. Since the ouster of Saddam Hussein, between one million and two million Shi'i Muslims have made the pilgrimage each year. A large number of pilgrims travel to the site from Iran, a nation with a Shi'i majority.

Sunni Muslims are a minority in Iraq, but Sunnis made up a majority of the membership of Hussein's Ba'th Party. The Sunni Arabs ruled Iraq with an iron fist. They are now concerned that they are rapidly losing political control of the country. Most Kurds are also Sunni. During Hussein's regime, the Sunni Kurds were persecuted by their Sunni Arab brothers. This was because of ethnic issues, not religion. Many Sunni Arabs prefer to separate religion from the national political agenda.

The Grand Ayatollah Ali Muhammad al-Sistani

The most powerful Shi'i religious leader in Iraq today is the Grand Ayatollah Ali Muhammad al-Sistani. He is one of only five living grand ayatollahs, the highest rank in the Shi'i religious leadership structure. Millions of Iraqi Shi'is follow his teachings and instructions. Al-Sistani prefers to study the scholarly and spiritual aspects of Islam rather than to engage in politics. He lives in well-guarded privacy at a housing compound in the holy city of Najaf. He has often been praised for his moderate views, and his leadership will be critical for maintaining Islamic unity in Iraq.

A Christian Minority

There has been a Christian presence in the area that is now Iraq for many hundreds of years. Several Christian monks settled in the area near Mosul in the fourth century. The oldest Syrian Orthodox Christian monastery in northern Iraq was established in the mid-500s. This ancient complex, which is dedicated to Saint Matthew, is located just a few miles from Mosul. Christian pilgrims visiting the site sometimes collect soil from the monastery grounds because they believe it is holy and will bless them.

The city of Mosul also contains many ancient Christian churches. The oldest, the Church of Saint Peter, was founded in the ninth century. This church contains many valuable archaeological items.

Today, about 3 percent of Iraqis are Christian. They belong to a variety of Catholic, Orthodox, and Protestant churches. Though Christians have a long history in Iraq, they have also been persecuted for many centuries. Many Iraqi Christians have scattered to other places across the world.

The Syrian Orthodox Church of St. Thomas is located in Baghdad. It was damaged by bombs in 2004.

A Rich Culture

THROUGHOUT HISTORY, FEW REGIONS OF THE WORLD HAVE
been exposed to as many cultures as modern Iraq. Each group
that swept through what is now Iraq contributed to the culture of this diverse nation.

Opposite: **Some Iraqi women leave only their faces and hands uncovered.**

Close Friends

Iraqis in general are a generous, friendly, and talkative people.
They make friends quickly and easily, and they nurture those
friendships with frequent contact. They are especially loyal
to family and friends and seldom say no to a friend's request.
Often, after they agree to a request, they will add the phrase
In'shallah, meaning that they will fulfill the request if God is
willing. If God is not willing, then the request goes unfulfilled.
This is always more acceptable than saying no.

Friendship and generosity are central to Iraqi life.

Rest in Peace

The teachings of Islam determine burial customs in Iraq. It is believed that with the last breath, a Muslim's soul departs from the body and enters paradise. After a person dies, the body is washed, normally by a family member, and wrapped in white cloth. The body is laid in a grave, with the right side facing Mecca. If possible, the burial occurs before sundown on the day of death.

Iraqis love to talk and become quite animated while engaged in conversation. Discussions almost always involve a great deal of hand and arm movements. It is also common for Iraqis to talk quite loudly, interrupt each other, and repeat themselves to emphasize a point. Emotional outbursts are normal. Iraqis often touch each other on the arm while talking to members of the same sex. Touching members of the opposite sex is taboo, including shaking hands, hugging, or giving a pat on the back.

All in the Family

Families are the center of the Iraqi social universe. Family members, even distant relatives, are expected to maintain total loyalty to the family. Speaking badly of any member of the family is unacceptable. Behavior that brings shame to the family must be avoided at all costs. If a family member needs financial help, Iraqis make every possible attempt to help that person.

A traditional Iraqi family may be quite large. A household could include a husband and wife as well as all unmarried children, married sons with their wives and children, and the husband's parents. When parents are unable to care for

themselves, they traditionally move into the home of their oldest son. Caring for their elderly parents late in their lives is considered a privilege in Iraqi society, not a responsibility.

Fathers are the center of power in an Iraqi family. They are primarily responsible for earning the family income. Fathers are the major source of discipline for children. Mothers are expected to take care of the children and are the major source of love and affection. As a result, grown children, especially men, adore their mothers and treat them with great respect.

In Iraqi cities, most houses have large rooms and high ceilings. The houses usually have balconies in the front and the back and a patio on the roof where people can sleep during the hot summers.

Some Iraqis wear Western-style clothes at their wedding. A joyous feast follows the ceremony.

The birth of a child brings joy to a family and is openly celebrated. Parents adore their children while they are young and spoil them with many gifts. As children grow, they accept increasing responsibility around the house. Misbehavior, especially by girls, is unacceptable. Boys are given much more latitude in how they behave. Children are taught to show great respect for elders and to never interrupt adults.

Selecting a Spouse

In both Kurdish and Arab cultures, most marriages are arranged. Normally, the mothers of future husbands and wives discuss and negotiate the selection of a spouse. The future bride and groom do not date. Photos are sometimes exchanged, and both the boy and the girl may reject their mother's choice. The importance of family in marriage is frequently reflected in the fact that cousins, even first cousins, commonly marry.

The Iraq Museum

The Iraq Museum was founded in Baghdad in 1920 when the modern state of Iraq was created. As the nation grew, so did the reputation of the museum. By the year 2000, it contained more than half a million artifacts. The collection included everything from prehistoric artifacts to recent Islamic objects. Gallery displays showcased some of the world's greatest cultures.

During the Iraq War, the museum suffered substantial damage. It is estimated that perhaps 15,000 valuable pieces were stolen, including a marble sculpture of a woman's head that dates back to 3000 B.C. The head has since been found, and Iraq and the international art community are working to recover the other missing treasures.

Excellence in the Arts

Iraq has a lengthy history of intellectual accomplishment in writing, art, and music. Until recently, its population was among the best educated in the Middle East. The country contains many libraries, museums, and galleries that house some of the world's finest collections of art and artifacts. Unfortunately, recent military conflict, looters, and bad leaders have hurt the arts.

Reading and writing have been significant aspects of Iraqi culture for centuries. In Islamic societies, reading is critical to religious training. For many children, the ability to read the Qur'an, which is written in classical Arabic, is an important goal.

Children studying the Qur'an. Parts of the Qur'an are written in rhyme.

Writing It Down

The history of many ancient cultures has been lost because those societies did not have a system of writing. Experts believe that the first system of writing, called cuneiform, was developed by the Sumerians by 3000 B.C. The Sumerians used a wedge-shaped tool to inscribe symbols on stone, metal, ivory, and clay tablets. Clay tablets were used most often because of the softness of the clay.

Thousands of cuneiform tablets have been discovered and preserved. The clay tablets vary in size from 1 square inch (6 sq cm) to 1 square foot (930 sq cm) and occasionally larger. Surviving examples of cuneiform writing include legal codes, poems, medical writings, prayers, and contracts. The *Epic of Gilgamesh* tells the story of the ancient adventures of the historical king of Uruk. It is believed to be the oldest surviving written story on earth.

Libraries in Iraq are full of important scholarly works written by Iraqis. The most popular literature is a collection of writings known as *A Thousand and One Nights*, or *Arabian Nights*. This collection of more than two hundred myths, legends, poetry, and history has become a favorite all over the world. Many of the stories take place in Baghdad. These tales include such well-known characters as Scheherazade, Aladdin, Ali Baba and the Forty Thieves, and Sinbad the Sailor. Many of the stories revolve around magical events, and most have a moral, or lesson about life.

Jawad Salim

Jawad Salim (1920–1961) was born into a family of noted artists. From early in his life, it was clear that he would become a talented sculptor and painter. Salim studied art in Paris, Rome, and Baghdad. He and a group of colleagues founded the Baghdad Modern Art Group in 1951. Salim is often considered the father of modern Iraqi sculpture. His best-known work is the Monument for Liberty, one of Iraq's most famous landmarks.

The Kurdish and Turkmen minorities in Iraq are also successful in the arts. Both groups are noted for their poetry and storytelling. Kurdish carpets are considered works of art by many people. Turkmen artisans create some of the world's most beautiful gold and silver jewelry. Hand-embroidered clothing is a tradition among both Kurds and Turkmen.

The Kurds are famous for their rugs. They often include both geometric and animals shapes.

Music is a central feature in the lives of most Iraqis. The most important musical instruments are flutes, drums, and the oud, or "ut-ut," a string instrument similar to the guitar. Ballads reflecting on romance and love are popular. Iraqis also enjoy folkloric dancing and fast-paced instrumental music. Many younger Iraqis prefer Western music, including hip-hop and rock.

Yair Dalal plays the oud in a concert. The oud is played like a guitar though the sound is distinctly different.

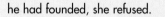

The Thrill of Competition

The most popular sport in Iraq is soccer. Soccer fields can be found all over Iraq, although many are in poor condition. If a soccer field is not available, players create a makeshift field on vacant lots, streets, or just about anywhere else. Almost every Iraqi boy dreams of playing on the national team. Young Iraqis will play barefoot on dirt fields with any type of ball they can find.

Miracle on Grass

After the downfall of Saddam Hussein's government in 2003, Iraq quickly assembled an Olympic soccer team with the goal

The Survivor

Runner Iman Sabeeh is a national hero to many Iraqis. During the 1980s, she set Iraqi records in the 400- and 800-meter races that still stand today. Each year from 1980 to 1987, Sabeeh was voted the most popular female athlete in the country.

Sabeeh survived during a dangerous time when Saddam Hussein's volatile son, Uday, controlled Olympic sports in Iraq. He had athletes tortured and even killed if they lost. Uday refused to allow Sabeeh to travel to the 1984 Los Angeles Olympics. When Uday tried to force her to join a new sports team that

he had founded, she refused.

Sabeeh flourished after the ouster of Hussein. In 2004, she was chosen as the only female member of the National Olympic Committee of Iraq. At the Summer Olympics that year in Athens, Greece, Sabeeh proudly marched with the Iraqi team in the opening ceremonies.

of playing in the 2004 Olympics in Athens, Greece. At the time, most soccer analysts believed Iraq had little chance of qualifying for the Olympics. The team lacked the proper equipment and training. Security issues prevented other teams from traveling to Iraq to compete. But the soccer analysts had seriously underestimated the basic skills and work ethic of the Iraqi players. Failure was not an option for them.

A team of Shi'i, Sunni, and Kurdish players set out to defy the odds. In May 2004, the Iraqis pulled off a stunning upset of Saudi Arabia. For the first time in Iraqi history, the soccer team qualified to play in the Olympics. At the Olympics, Iraq's team surprised Portugal, Costa Rica, and Australia, earning the right to advance to the medal round. Although they did not win a medal, they finished fourth overall. This achievement on the soccer fields of Greece lifted the spirits and pride of Iraqis all over the world.

The Iraqi national soccer team returns to Baghdad after coming in fourth at the Athens Olympics. Their many wins brought cheering Iraqis out into the streets.

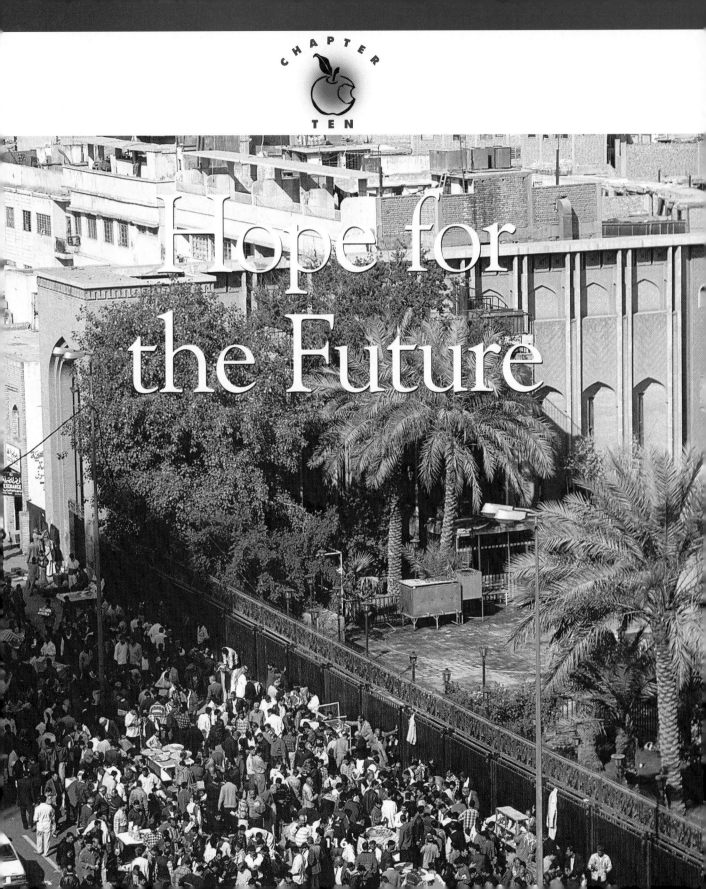

Hope for the Future

T HE PATTERNS OF DAILY LIFE IN IRAQ HAVE BEEN SERIOUSLY interrupted by wars, economic sanctions, occupation by foreign troops, and civil unrest. A normal life has been denied to at least two generations of Iraqi citizens. They are not able to do the things people around the world take for granted. They struggle to find jobs, feed their children, and provide their families with adequate health care. Each day, Iraqis' lives are in danger, and the major goal for many is to survive to the next day. A normal pattern of daily life will not return until a legitimate government can guarantee security and safety to its citizens.

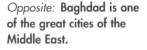

Opposite: **Baghdad is one of the great cities of the Middle East.**

Baghdad was severely damaged during the Iraq War.

Even though times are difficult, there are certain aspects of life that must go on. Citizens need a place to live, food to eat, clothes to wear, and a job to provide for their families.

Housing is in short supply in Iraq. Most Iraqis live in large cities such as Baghdad, Mosul, and Basra, where houses are built from concrete blocks with tile roofs. Although many Iraqis own their own homes, new arrivals to the cities are frequently housed in crowded apartments. A few wealthy Iraqis live in mansions in private suburbs on the edge of the cities. In rural areas, mud-brick homes of two or three rooms are common.

Sadr City, in northeastern Baghdad, is one of the poorest areas of Iraq. After the Iraq War began, the water supply became polluted, the sewage system was damaged, and the electricity was only on a few hours a day.

Today, many Iraqis are doing without basic services. Since the end of the Iraq War, many have gone without a regular supply of electricity or safe drinking water. Difficulties with sewage and garbage disposal are also common. Without these services, people cannot return to the normal patterns of life.

Many houses were destroyed during the Iraq War, so some families have had to crowd in together.

War Games

Children growing up in Iraq over the past twenty-five years have been frequently exposed to war and violence. Many have lost their innocence and their hope. When their teachers ask them to draw pictures, they draft images of tanks, guns, and bombed-out buildings and cars. Few draw the normal pictures of childhood: animals, flowers, toys, or friends.

Because children frequently copy what they see in the real world, many Iraqi children play war games. They make pretend guns, plant imaginary bombs made from cardboard boxes, and plot attacks on enemies. Iraq's future lies in the hands of these children. Only when their safety and security is improved will they be able to lead normal lives and play normal games.

A Kurdish family gathers for a meal in Mosul. The long afternoon meal brings everyone together.

A Daily Routine

Although food shortages are common throughout Iraq, families still gather for three meals a day. Iraqis love meat, but for many families meat prices are too high. Bread, rice, vegetables, and fruit provide most of their nourishment.

In more traditional and in most poor households, meals are served on the floor. A cloth is spread over the carpet,

Time to Eat

Breakfast is eaten early in the morning before everyone leaves for work or school. It is usually a light meal of bread with cheese or eggs and some fruit. The main meal of the day is served between 2:00 and 4:00 P.M.

This meal usually includes rice, vegetables, meat (lamb is the favorite), bread, and a rich dessert. The evening meal is commonly eaten around 8:00 P.M. and may consist of leftovers, a sandwich, or a plate of fruit.

and the dishes are placed in a central location. Mealtime is family time, and everyone is expected to attend. The large midafternoon meal is consumed at a leisurely pace, and good conversation is a part of the experience. Coffee or tea is usually served with sweet desserts at the end of the meal.

The Fast of Ramadan

Eating and drinking habits during the Islamic month of Ramadan change dramatically. For that one month, no food or water may be consumed from sunrise to sunset. Exceptions are made for pregnant women, children, travelers, and those who are ill. Muslims engage in fasting to experience how it feels to be hungry and thirsty. They believe it makes them more compassionate for the poor and strengthens their faith in God. When

Ramadan falls during the summer months, the daily fasting period may last up to sixteen hours.

To prepare for the fast, Iraqi Muslims get out of bed before dawn and eat. This meal is call *suhur*. They eat foods such as grains, nuts, dates, and bananas, which digest slowly and delay the feelings of hunger. The fast is broken at sundown with a meal termed *iftar*. This festive meal includes soups, bread, meats, vegetables, and fruit.

Generally speaking, the Kurds and Turkmen in northern Iraq dress differently than the country's Arab population. Both ethnic groups use much brighter colors and mix the colors freely. Women wear long dresses over loose-fitting pantaloons, jackets, and head scarves. The men wear baggy pants with a shirt and jacket. On their heads they place a skullcap and a neatly folded turban. Because the Kurds are a strongly tribal society, men frequently wear clothes with colors that represent their tribe or political party.

At celebrations, Kurds often wear their brightly colored traditional clothes. At other times, younger Kurds are more likely to wear Western fashions.

Some Iraqi women cover
their heads, but others do not.

In central Iraq, particularly in Sunni areas, many men wear Western-style clothes. The more traditional men wear *thawbs* (long shirts that go down to the ankles) with *kufiyah* (skull-caps) and *gutra* (head scarves). The scarves are held in place by *egals* (cloth twisted into a rope).

Some Sunni women and almost all Shi'i women wear clothing that covers their entire bodies. An *abaya* (a long, black gown) is worn over a blouse and pantaloons. Many women wear scarves over their hair, and some older women wear veils over their faces. These women feel that it is improper to reveal

Some professional women, like this civil engineer in Baghdad, wear Western-style clothes.

the shape of the female body. Sunni businesswomen sometimes wear Western fashions, but only conservative styles.

Many teenagers and younger children wear Western-style clothes, particularly in the cities. But the girls never wear the revealing clothing that many young American girls wear.

Public Holidays in Iraq

In Iraq, nonreligious holidays are based on the 365-day Georgian calendar used in the West. Religious holidays are based on the 354-day Islamic calendar. As a result, religious holidays fall on different dates in the Western calendar each year.

Nonreligious Holidays

January 1	New Year's Day
January 6	Army Day
February 8	Anniversary of the Revolution
April 17	World Food Day
May 1	Labor Day
July 14	National Day
July 17	Ba'th Revolution Day
August 8	Peace Day

Religious Holidays

Eid al-Adha (Festival of Sacrifice)
Muharram (Islamic New Year)
Ashura (anniversary of the death of Hussein)
Muhammad's Birthday
Start of Ramadan
Eid al-Fitr (End of Ramadan)

Finding a Job

When the regime of Saddam Hussein collapsed, many people lost their jobs. The army and police force were disbanded, leaving thousands of men unemployed. Today, unemployment rates are estimated to be between 30 and 50 percent. Even those who have jobs are frequently underemployed. This means they are overqualified for low-paying jobs. An example is a medical doctor who now is a taxi driver. It is almost impossible for young people entering the job market to find work.

Not only are jobs hard to find, but wages are also declining. The median income in Iraq was estimated at $255 per year in 2003. A year later, the median income had slipped to $144. In a recent survey by the Iraqi government and the United Nations, one-fourth of Iraqis stated that they lived in poverty. Ninety-six percent of the surveyed group said that they received food rations.

Iraqi men wait in line for job interviews. Jobs are hard to come by, which leads to frustration and anger.

A Questionable Future

Iraq has given the world some of its greatest civilizations. It is a country that is blessed with incredible reserves of oil and natural gas. The valleys of the Tigris and the Euphrates rivers have the potential to support extensive agriculture. Yet the people of Iraq have suffered great injustices. They hold on to a tiny thread of hope that the future will be better. Many outside observers also hope for a brighter future for the Iraqi people. Iraqis deserve to have that hope become a reality. *In'shallah!*

Forty percent of Iraqis are fourteen years old or younger. Given Iraq's tumultuous recent history, their future remains uncertain.

Timeline

Iraqi History		World History
Mesopotamian culture begins.	ca. 10,000 B.C. 1	
Sumerian civilization thrives in Mesopotamia.	3500–2350 B.C.	2500 B.C. Egyptians build the Pyramids and the Sphinx in Giza.
Sargon establishes the Akkadian Empire.	2300s B.C.	
Hammurabi becomes king of Babylonia.	1792 B.C.	
The Assyrians control Babylonia.	1600–609 B.C.	
The reign of King Nebuchadnezzar II begins.	605 B.C.	
The Persian Empire gains control of Mesopotamia.	538 B.C.	563 B.C. The Buddha is born in India.
Alexander the Great conquers Mesopotamia.	331 B.C.	
		A.D. 313 The Roman emperor Constantine recognizes Christianity.
The Arabs invade.	A.D. 633	610 The Prophet Muhammad begins preaching a new religion called Islam.
Caliph Ali is murdered.	661	
The Abbasid Dynasty is established.	750	
		1054 The Eastern (Orthodox) and Western (Roman) Churches break apart.
		1066 William the Conqueror defeats the English in the Battle of Hastings.
		1095 Pope Urban II proclaims the First Crusade.
		1215 King John seals the Magna Carta.
The Mongols invade and destroy Baghdad.	1258	1300s The Renaissance begins in Italy.
		1347 The Black Death sweeps through Europe.
		1453 Ottoman Turks capture Constantinople, conquering the Byzantine Empire.
		1492 Columbus arrives in North America.

Iraqi History

The Ottoman Empire takes control of Mesopotamia.	1534
British troops invade Mesopotamia during World War I.	1914
The British are given a mandate to govern Iraq.	1920
The British appoint Faisal I as king of Iraq.	1921
The boundaries for the modern state of Iraq are established.	1925
Oil is discovered in Iraq.	1927
Iraq becomes independent.	1932
The Iraqi monarchy is overthrown in a military coup.	1958
Iraq's oil industry is nationalized.	1972
Saddam Hussein becomes president/dictator of Iraq.	1979
The Iran-Iraq War begins.	1980
The Gulf War begins.	1991
Saddam Hussein is ousted during the Iraq War.	2003
Iraq holds elections	2005

World History

1500s	The Reformation leads to the birth of Protestantism.
1776	The Declaration of Independence is signed.
1789	The French Revolution begins.
1865	The American Civil War ends.
1914	World War I breaks out.
1917	The Bolshevik Revolution brings communism to Russia.
1929	Worldwide economic depression begins.
1939	World War II begins, following the German invasion of Poland.
1945	World War II ends.
1957	The Vietnam War starts.
1969	Humans land on the moon.
1975	The Vietnam War ends.
1979	Soviet Union invades Afghanistan.
1983	Drought and famine in Africa.
1989	The Berlin Wall is torn down, as communism crumbles in Eastern Europe.
1991	Soviet Union breaks into separate states.
1992	Bill Clinton is elected U.S. president.
2000	George W. Bush is elected U.S. president.
2001	Terrorists attack World Trade Towers, New York, and the Pentagon, Washington, D.C.
2003	The U.S. invades Iraq.

Fast Facts

Official name: Republic of Iraq

Capital: Baghdad

Official languages: Arabic, Kurdish

Baghdad

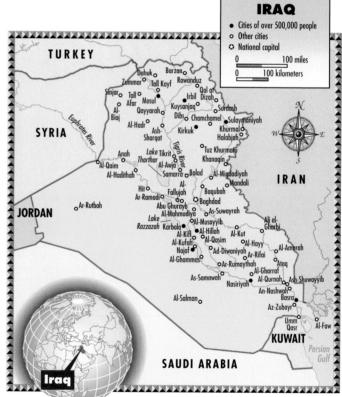

Iraq's flag

Date palms

Official religion:	Islam
Year of founding:	1932
National anthems:	"Matwini" (Arab), "Ey Regib" (Kurd)
Area:	169,235 square miles (438,317 sq km)
Latitude and longitude of country's geographic center:	33°N, 44°E
Bordering countries:	Iran, Jordan, Kuwait, Saudi Arabia, Syria, Turkey
Highest elevation:	Haji Ibrahim, at 11,834 feet (3,607 m)
Lowest elevation:	Sea level along the Persian Gulf
Highest average temperature:	93°F (32.7°C)
Lowest average temperature:	54°F (12.2°C)
Average precipitation:	6 inches (15 cm)
Major rivers:	Tigris, Euphrates, Shatt al-Arab
Largest lake:	Lake Tharthar
National population:	26,074,906 (July 2005 est.)

Population of largest cities:		
	Baghdad	5,605,000
	Mosul	1,739,000
	Basra	1,337,000
	Irbil	839,000
	Kirkuk	728,000

The ruins of ancient Babylon

Famous landmarks: ▶ *Shrine of Hussein*, Karbala

▶ *Mutawakkil Mosque with Malwiya Minaret*, Samarra

▶ *Ashur (Qal'at Sherqat)*, near Mosul

▶ *Hatra*, near Mosul

▶ *Martyr's Monument*, Baghdad

▶ *Baghdad Museum*, Baghdad

▶ *Ziggurat of Ur*, near Nasiriyah

Industry: Iraq's industrial sector is poorly developed. Oil refining, petrochemicals, and natural-gas processing dominate manufacturing activities. But production is well below capacity and plagued with many problems such as old and damaged equipment. The processing of food and beverages is important locally, and cement production for the construction industry is found in several regions of Iraq.

Currency: The new Iraqi dinar. In 2005, one U.S. dollar equaled 1,470 dinars.

Weights and measures: Metric system

Literacy rate: 40%

Currency

An Iraqi schoolgirl

Ibrahim al-Jafari

Common words and phrases in Iraqi Arabic:

Shu ismak?	What is your name?
Marhaba	Hello
Ma' assalama	Goodbye
Minfadlik	Please
Shukran	Thank you

Famous Iraqis:

Ali ibn Abu Talib (598–661)
Fourth caliph of Islam

Hammurabi (? –1750 B.C.)
Ruler of Babylon who developed a famous legal code

Hussein ibn Ali Abu Talib (629–680)
Shi'i martyr

Saddam Hussein (1937–)
President and dictator of Iraq

Ibrahim al-Jafari (1947–)
Prime minister of Iraqi transitional government

Nebuchadnezzar II (615–562 B.C.)
Powerful Babylonian king

Jawad Salim (1920–1961)
Iraqi sculptor and painter

Ali Muhammad al-Sistani (1930–)
Shi'i religious leader

To Find Out More

Nonfiction

▶ Bryant, Tamera. *The Life and Times of Hammurabi*. Hockessin, Del.: Mitchell Lane Publishers, 2005.

▶ Richie, Jason. *Iraq and the Fall of Saddam Hussein*. Minneapolis: Oliver Press, 2003.

Fiction

▶ McCaughrean, Geraldine. *1001 Arabian Nights*. New York: Oxford University Press, 2000.

Articles

▶ Boulat, Alexandra. "Baghdad before the Bombs," *National Geographic* (June 2003): 52–69.

▶ DiGiovanni, Janine. "Reaching for Power," *National Geographic* (June 2004): 2–35.

Web Sites

▶ **Iraq Map-2004**
http://www.sunship.com/mideast/
info/maps/iraq-map.html
*For a variety of current and detailed
color maps that show oil facilities,
ethnic and religious distributions, population density, and the city of Baghdad*

▶ **Time for Kids Online**
http://timeforkids.com/TFK/specials/
iraq/0,8805,424876,00.html
*For maps, a timeline, and
information about the country's
history and conflicts*

Embassy

▶ **Embassy of the Republic of Iraq**
1801 P Street, NW
Washington, DC 20036
202/483-7500

Index

Page numbers in *italics* indicate illustrations.

Syrian Orthodox Church of St.
    Thomas, *103*
    Zakat (Fourth Pillar of Islam), 98
religious holidays, 125
reptilian life, 33–34, *33*
resources map, *71*
rockrose bushes, 32
Rumaila oil field, 19, 56, 71

S

Sabeeh, Iman, 114
Sadr City, *93*, *118*
Salat (Second Pillar of Islam), 97–98
Salim, Jawad, 112, *112*
al-Salman, 27
sand gazelles, 35
sandstorms, 13, 26, 27, *27*, 37
Sargon I of Akkad, 11, *11*, 42
Sassanid Dynasty, 46, 47
Saudi Arabia, 19, 21, 47, 48, 93, 94,
    94, 98–99, *99*, 106, 115
saw-scale vipers, 34
Sawm (Third Pillar of Islam), 98
scorpions, *31*, 34
scribes, 42
Sennacherib (Assyrian king), 11, 44
September 11 attacks, 57
Shahadah (First Pillar of Islam), 96
Shatt al-Arab, 19, 20, 29
Shi'i Muslims, 15, 48, 49, 50, 59, 61,
    62, 63, 64, 65, 84, 93, 95, 96, 97,
    101, 102, *102*, 115
al-Sistani, Ali Muhammad, 102,
    102, 133
soccer, 114–115, *115*
sports, 114–115, *115*
Square of the Unknown Soldier, 8

Strait of Hormuz, *18*
suhur (Ramadan meal), 121
Sulaymaniyah, 82
Suleiman the Magnificent, 11, 51, *51*
Sumerian Empire, 11, *40*
Sumerians, 10, 11, 41–42, *41*, *42*, 43,
    111, *111*
Sunni Muslims, 15, 48, 50, 51, 55,
    59, 62, 63, 64, 65, 84, *84*, 85, 86,
    93, 96, 102, 115, 123
Syria, 19, 21, *21*, 39, 48, 54, 59,
    76, 85
Syrian Orthodox Church, 103, *103*

T

Tamerlane (Mongol conqueror), 50
Taurus Mountain range, 24
terrorism, 57
textile industry, 75, 77, *77*
thawbs (clothing), 123
A Thousand and One Nights
    (story collection), 111
Tigris River, 10, 17, *17*, 18–19, 20, 23,
    24, 26, 29, *29*, 36, 38, 39, 41, 42,
    66, 74–75, 76, 81–82, 84, 127
Tikrit, 61, 84
topographical map, *19*
transportation, 27, 61
Turkey, 19, 20, 23, 24, 28, 39, 76, *76*,
    85, 86, 89
Turkish Petroleum Company (TPC),
    70, 71
Turkmen, 62, 83, 86, 112, 122

U

Umayyad Dynasty, 48, 101

Umm Qasr, 19
United Kindgom. *See* Great Britain.
United Nations, 56
United States, 15, *15*, 38, 56, 57, 60,
    61, *62*, 70, 85
University of Baghdad, *91*
Ur, 11, 42

V

villages, 22, 26, 36, 61

W

wadis (dry streambeds), 12, 22
water, 10, 12, *16*, 17, *17*, 23, *23*,
    24, 26, 32, 38, *38*, 39, 41, 45,
    74, 76, *76*, 77, 81–82,
    119, *118*
weights and measures, 70
wildlife. *See* animal life; plant life.
women, 63, *63*, *104*, 114, *114*, 122,
    122, 123–124, *123*, *124*
World War I, 52, 53, 70, 85
wormwood, 36

Y

Yazid (caliph), 48, 49

Z

Zagros Mountains, 13, *13*, *20*, 24
Zakat (Fourth Pillar of Islam), 98
Zubair field, 71

Meet the Authors

BYRON AUGUSTIN is the Piper Professor of Geography at Texas State University in San Marcos, Texas. His love for geography has given him a passion for traveling. He has visited forty-nine of the fifty United States, twenty-six of Mexico's thirty-one states, and eight Canadian provinces. Augustin has also visited fifty-four countries on five of the seven continents.

Augustin is the author of *Qatar, Bolivia, United Arab Emirates, Panama,* and *Paraguay* for the Enchantment of the World series as well as six books in Scholastic's A to Z country book series. He is also a professional photographer. More than twelve hundred of his photos have been published worldwide. His photos have been featured by the National Geographic Society and in *Encyclopedia Britannica, Outdoor Life,* and scores of magazines and books, including more than a dozen Enchantment of the World books.

Augustin has worked to try to improve relations between the United States and the Arab and Islamic world. He served as the state director for the Texas Committee on U.S.-Arab Relations and has traveled frequently to the Middle East. Because of his tireless efforts, he received the Award of Distinction from the Arab-American Cultural and Community Center of Houston, Texas.

JAKE KUBENA is a geography teacher in Wimberley, Texas. He earned a bachelor of science degree in geography from Texas State University–San Marcos in 2003 and is working toward a master's degree.

Kubena has edited many geography books, including *Panama* and *Paraguay* in the Enchantment of the World series and *Dominican Republic*, *England*, *Greece*, *Indonesia*, and *Argentina* in the A to Z countries series. He is also coauthor of *Turkey* in the A to Z series. Kubena enjoys traveling and has frequented Mexico since childhood. He has also traveled in the United States and Europe.

Photo Credits